How Pierre
and I
Saved the
Civilized
World

Also by Gary Lautens

LAUGHING WITH LAUTENS
TAKE MY FAMILY . . . PLEASE!
NO SEX, PLEASE . . . WE'RE MARRIED

GARY LAUTENS

How Pierre and I Saved the Civilized World

Cartoons by
Duncan Macpherson

(∏) Methuen

Toronto   New York   London   Sydney   Auckland

Cartoons by Macpherson reprinted with permission
—Toronto Star Syndicate
Design: Fortunato Aglialoro

Canadian Cataloguing in Publication Data

Lautens, Gary
    How Pierre and I saved the civilized world

A selection of the author's columns from the Toronto Star.
ISBN 0-458-98720-4 (bound). – ISBN 0-458-98600-3 (pbk.)

1. Trudeau, Pierre Elliott, 1919–   – Cartoons,
satire, etc.   2. Canadian wit and humor (English)*
3. Canada – Politics and government – 1963–   –
Anecdotes, facetiae, satire, etc. * I. Macpherson,
Duncan Ian, 1924–   II. The Toronto star.   III. Title.

FC626.T78L38 1984   971.064′4′0924   C84-098907-5
F1034.3.T78L38 1984

Printed and bound in Canada

1 2 3 4   84   88 87 86 85

4

Contents

PM could be part-time postie on world travels
Iron bars do not a prison make Quebeckers find
"I didn't raise a son of mine to hang around Parliament"
I have some words Trudeau could use . . .

Chapter 4: Domesticity / 50

Chapter 5: Election 1972 / 62

Chapter 6: Election 1974 / 75

Nixon wasn't talking about Trudeau at all!
Getting the scoop at 24 Sussex Drive
Trudeau (sob) wastes our best rude words
Maryon, come home to 24 Sussex Drive
"Tell it like it isn't" people beg Trudeau
Trudeau's private life leaves us all guessing
Trudeau's troubles can't help Joe Clark
Was Trudeau right in saying "Hello"?

Chapter 7: The World Stage / 95

Pierre, eat peanuts at the White House
It's our duty to live beyond our means
Here's the sequel to Cinderella's story
That was no face-lift, just a lift in spirits
Was Maggie discussing Pierre with Barbra?
But Pierre, the bank wants cash
What is Pierre's secret of youth?
Put Pierre where he belongs—abroad
Pierre lifts a finger, Canada's letter editors cower
Tories love Trudeau but Grits need Joe
If PM is defeated, what will Trudeau-haters do?
Can Begin bring peace to Canada?

Chapter 8: Interruption / 117

Trudeau on Toronto has us speechless
Help poor Pierre: Get a unity tattoo
Wrong sometimes but often right
Pierre? Pierre Who?
We're on the brink of a new shortage—the insult crisis
Here's what the parties say—now you can ignore them
Oh for day when Joe Clark turns guns on Brezhnev
Goodbye, goodbye to humble pie: It's a Liberal feast again

Chapter 9: Resurrection / 133

With the mess Tories left, will poor Liberals need time?
Canadians aren't quite ready to parle the Frenglish language
How to protect the innocent
Poor PM! There's just no pleasing some newspapers
What gift should Peter give Pierre?
Pierre must pine for his paperwork
Pierre's in for a surprise
Constitution comedy just a barrel of belly laughs
"Lady Jane could feel all resistance draining away"
In the name of peace . . .

Epilogue / 153

Introduction

Running a big country isn't easy but, fortunately, Pierre Trudeau never had to do it alone. From the time he took office as Prime Minister in 1968 'til he cleaned out his desk in June of 1984, Mr. Trudeau always had the press to give him advice, solve complicated problems and show him The True Way.

Speaking for myself, I know I've given him tips in print on everything from how he should talk to Richard Nixon ("talk into the pen stand") to how he should kiss on the campaign trail ("use a grapefruit if your pucker starts to droop"). And not once, I'm proud to say, did I ever send the PM a bill for my counsel.

If a prime minister can't turn to a columnist to solve unemployment or explain the mysteries of Barbra Streisand, who can he turn to?

What follows are columns written about Pierre Trudeau. They appeared originally in the Toronto Star and are dated and presented here in chronological order.

One of my favorites is a July 18, 1968, assessment by my mother of the then relatively unknown new Prime Minister. Bertha based her comments on the horoscope and, looking back, she was pretty accurate with one exception—her prediction that PET would get bored with politics and leave office after "five to eight years." Mr. Trudeau proved more durable than the stars, as perceived one afternoon in our family kitchen, indicated.

Another column that has a special place with me is dated March 31, 1977. A friend of mine named Ray Staples was discussing the breakup of the Trudeau marriage while we were on a TV set and she said something I considered poignant. "For years we wondered what happened to Cinderella after she rode off into the sunset with Prince Charming. Now we know." Her remark was the inspiration for what you see on page

The material presented here does not include the last year of the Trudeau administration. The reason for that is I stopped writing a daily column at the beginning of 1982. I'm sure it's only a coincidence but not much later, Mr. Trudeau decided to leave politics. Maybe he was just weary, or maybe he found managing the nation alone too heavy a responsibility.

Chapter 1: Charisma

With opposition like this Trudeau should be cinch

EVERYONE has been wondering why Pierre Trudeau took so long to make up his mind about running for the Liberal party leadership.

Some observers claimed he was being shy. Others suggested he was stalling for dramatic effect. But most admitted they just didn't know.

Now the story can be told.

Last week at Trudeau's headquarters I overheard two of his top aides talking. This is a transcript of what was said.

"Can we announce that Trudeau is going to run?"

"Not yet. We still haven't heard from you-know-who. One word from him could upset the applecart."

"Why doesn't he come out and make a statement so we can either go home or get started on our campaign? We'll need buttons, slogans, posters and a million other things."

"I know. I think you-know-who gets a kick out of keeping us waiting like this."

"How do things look otherwise?"

"Pretty good. Trudeau seems to reach intellectuals yet he's got a liberal background which also appeals to the working man."

"Being a dashing bachelor won't hurt his chances, either. It gives him an image of glamor which the women like."

"We realize that. And the publicity he got out of the divorce and homosexuality bill couldn't have come at a better time."

"All the papers have been carrying Trudeau stories—editorials, biographies, interpretive columns. It's astonishing the way he's captured the imagination of the nation."

"It really is. Important people have been begging him for weeks to run for the leadership."

"We can't put them off much longer. There's another press conference scheduled later today. What can I say this time?"

"You'll just have to tell them that Pierre hasn't made up his mind yet. Tell them he has to check with his western supporters and confer with union leaders. Tell them anything—but don't make a commitment."

"Could I just hint that things look good or that Trudeau is overwhelmed by the support he's received from well-wishers?"

"Are you crazy? Until we hear from you-know-who we don't make a move."

"But the suspense is killing me."

Just then the telephone rang. One of the aides answered it. His face lit up. He clapped his hands. And he shouted to his friend:

"We're in! We're in! The campaign is on! Get those posters to the printers. Order 50,000 Trudeau buttons. Reserve a suite of rooms for convention week."

"But what about you-know-who?"

"He just came out in full opposition to Trudeau. He's supporting Paul Martin!"

"Thank God! Just cross your fingers and pray that Ralph Cowan doesn't change his mind."

February 19, 1968

NOTE: Ralph Cowan was a Liberal MP who was always identified in the press as a "maverick." He was known to march to a different drummer even when the Grits were leading the band.

Trudeau: Do the clothes make the prime minister?

HAVE YOU read that Pierre Trudeau won't say how much his campaign for the Liberal leadership is costing or who is providing the money?

There have been all sorts of guesses but I happen to know who is backing Trudeau. It's his tailor.

You've undoubtedly noticed how, after every Trudeau appearance, the newspapers carry very little about the justice minister's views on tax reform, medicare or economic stability.

If he says anything at all, it's pretty vague. In fact, Trudeau won't even disclose his age.

But we do get elaborate descriptions of Trudeau's clothes.

Sometimes he's "tweed-jacketed." Other times he's described as "mod."

We get front page photographs of his leather coat, with matching hat. We get angry editorials about whether or not he should be allowed to appear in the House of Commons without a tie.

Even his sandals have been extensively researched, described and interviewed.

In short, his wardrobe is an open book, even if his mind isn't.

Like most people, I didn't catch on for a while and then it hit me: What we are actually witnessing is a nation-wide fashion show.

As I understand it, the clothiers of the nation were getting their spring line ready and preparing their advertising budget when the Liberal leadership race was announced.

A tailor named Max said they'd be nuts to spend $500,000 for advertising when, for half of that, they could sponsor their own candidate in the campaign.

At first Max was booed down and his suggestion termed "impractical." Max explained that for years the government has been managed behind the scenes by steel tycoons, beer barons, newspaper publishers and mining magnates.

He convinced the tailors it was time for them to get in on a good thing.

Finally, they agreed.

They made up a suit (size 36, short) and told him to find a candidate.

Bob Winters was too tall; Allan MacEachen too plump; Paul Martin too old; Paul Hellyer too square; and so on.

As a last resort, they tried the suit on Trudeau and—wonder of wonders—it fit perfectly.

So they entered him in the race, gave him the funds he needed for a campaign, and promised to sell him all the clothes he modelled at a 50 per cent discount.

Everything has worked perfectly up till now.

Trudeau's clothes have been the talk of the country and voters are delighted that they've got at least one candidate they can look at rather than listen to.

What happens after the pre-Easter parade?

Trudeau may win the party leadership and, if he does, the clothing industry only insists that he take a strong stand on natural shoulders, pleats and turtleneck shirt for evening wear.

Otherwise, he's on his own.

March 22, 1968

A few ideas for
a bachelor PM...

FOR YEARS the leaders of major governments around the world have been married men. As a result, most of our legislation has favored the family unit.

However, Canada has scored a breakthrough by selecting a bachelor, Pierre Trudeau, for its highest office. And he's a self-styled "swinger."

Obviously, there are going to be some changes. In fact, according to my information, here are just a few of the "reforms" that Trudeau might have in mind.

Weekly boutonnieres for all bachelors over the age of 60 without a means test.

Legislation which will forbid landladies from knocking on your door at 4 o'clock in the morning and asking if there is anyone in the room with you.

Lower postal rates for cookies, handknit socks and homemade fudge sent to the bachelor by his mother.

An allowance of $100 a month for unwed fathers.

The immediate establishment of a Bachelor's Day in June when all single girls in the country will be required to wear a flower to the office—white for "no" and red for "yes."

Government loans for convertibles.

A government-sponsored shop in every major city where a bachelor may purchase champagne, smoking jackets, Jackie Gleason records, Sen Sen, etc. at reduced prices, thus cutting the high cost of loving.

Homes for wayward girls, and their telephone numbers.

The putting aside of a million acres of parkland and their

designation as lovers' lanes before the subdividers get their hands on it.

A minimum fine of $1,000 for any married couple who wants to invite a bachelor over for dinner and to meet somebody who is "loads of fun."

A seduction deduction for income tax purposes on the theory it costs more to keep 278 girl friends than one wife.

Incentive bonuses for newspapers which don't carry Ann Landers.

A central agency in every major city where a bachelor may go at any time of day or night and receive, free of charge, an antidote for his girl friend's brownies.

Guarantees from the immigration department to keep all single men with good profiles and builds like Harry Belafonte out of the country, regardless of race, creed or color.

Free passage and a year's keep for any girl between 18 and 29 who wants to migrate to Canada and can meet the rigid standard (36-23-36).

Wider park benches.

Revision of the criminal code to make it a capital offence to turn out a dress, bathing suit, etc. with a zipper that jams.

Establishment of a $10,000 prize for the inventor who comes up with an early warning device to detect jealous husbands and give the bachelor at least a 15-second headstart.

Anyone for a divorce?

April 8, 1968

Bobby meets Pierre: It's diplomacy a go-go

GENERALLY speaking, world leaders are older men. Ho Chi Minh, for example, is 78; de Gaulle is 77; Franco and Tito are 76; Mao is 75.

Even Kosygin (63) and LBJ (60 in August of this year) can hardly be classified as teenagers.

As a result, the public has a pretty stuffy picture of politicians. Sitting in arm chairs. Smoking cigars. And talking, talking, talking.

Anything else would puff them out.

However, the order is changing. Canada's Lester Pearson (71 next week) is being replaced by a swinging bachelor, Pierre Elliott Trudeau (48, going on 19) who is a thinking man's Frank Sinatra.

And, in the States, Bobby Kennedy (42) has a good chance to win the Democratic nomination and the presidency.

If Bobby makes it, can you imagine the groovy agenda when he and Trudeau get together for a day of talks?

I suspect their timetable might look something like this...

6 a.m.—Climb a small mountain before breakfast, Pierre and Bobby to discuss world gold crisis, if time permits.

9 a.m.—Breakfast.

9.15 a.m.—Five-mile run to nearest river. Loser to pay for breakfast and give tariff concession in next trade agreement.

10.30 to noon—Shoot rapids in canoes. During portage around Devil's Leap, Bobby to provide background on Viet Nam situation in return for French lessons from Pierre.

12 to 1 p.m.—Lunch. Bobby and Pierre to choose up sides for afternoon touch football game.

1 p.m.—Touch football. First half to be played under American rules, second half under Canadian. Loser promises to get haircut.

2 p.m.—Break to discuss international monetary situation, Red China, the U.S. nuclear policy, the problems of a divided Berlin. If possible, also overhaul continental defence system.

2.15 p.m.—Resume second half of touch football game. Loser to get Buffalo.

4 p.m.—Swim and rubdown. Bobby to rush home as soon as possible to baby-sit so Ethel can get hair done. Pierre to get on telephone to see if he can get a date for official state dinner at 7 p.m.

7 p.m.—State dinner. If possible, Pierre to explain to Bobby where Boston Bruins went wrong in Stanley Cup playoff with Montreal Canadiens. Bobby to review Middle East, air pollution and ask Pierre about old French-Canadian cure for diaper rash.

Midnight—Meet press and announce the success of day's meetings.

April 18, 1968

Can kissable Pierre
lick chapped lips?

CANADIANS have always been shy and reserved. Look at it this way.

Any people who recall the Saturday night hockey broadcasts on radio as the high point of their youth don't exactly qualify as swingers.

However, there's been a big change in the land of nice and slow. Canadians, it seems, are a pretty sexy lot after all.

In fact, the latest sport Canadians are playing is called Kiss The Prime Minister.

The idea of the game is to hide behind some bushes, or a Mountie, and jump out when Prime Minister Trudeau comes by and demand a kiss.

Usually, he obliges because (a) he's gallant (b) he has no wife to bug him about lipstick on his collar and (c) he enjoys that sort of thing.

Of course it's great public relations. Young ladies who have been kissed by the Prime Minister all say he's "terrific" and great in a clinch.

But how long can he keep this up?

There are approximately 10 million kissable females in Canada and now they all feel they're entitled to a kiss from the Prime Minister.

Some may be satisfied with a peck on the cheek. But most want a smack right on the mouth with a little squeeze thrown in as a bonus.

With his reputation as the "kissing prime minister" at stake, not to mention all those votes, Trudeau can hardly refuse.

Can you picture the poor fellow after a hard day's work. He flops in an easy chair and mutters: "My lips are killing me."

An aide begs him to save himself because he has to take his lips to another dozen public functions that evening.

"I can't do it," Trudeau sobs. "I've been kissed by girls with chapped lips, buck teeth, sharp noses and girls who have had liver for lunch.

"I've been grabbed by athletic girls who bent me over and popped the discs in my back.

"I've been cornered by old girls who didn't have time to put their teeth in and by teeny-boppers too excited to take their lollipops out.

"My lips have got to have a night off."

The aide will tell the Prime Minister to relax.

"That's easy for you to say," Trudeau will reply. "Have you ever been kissed by a steno who forgot to take a pencil out of her hair. I almost lost an eye.

"And there are housewives who have been married so long they don't remember how to kiss.

"Have you ever opened your eyes during a kiss and stared directly into another pair of eyes? I tell you I've got the shakes."

The aide reminds Trudeau the country is counting on him. He can't rest as long as there is a single (or married) woman unkissed.

"All right," Trudeau sighs. "But you better get me a grapefruit. I can't pucker up without some help.

"Boy, what I wouldn't give to shake hands with the next girl I meet."

April 24, 1968

Mother knows all about Trudeau

PIERRE TRUDEAU has everybody in the country guessing— everybody, that is, except my mother. She has him pegged.

Yesterday I was wondering out loud what kind of Prime Minister he would be.

"That's easy," mother said. "He'll be the boss. Libras are like that."

"Libras?"

"Trudeau's astrological sign, silly. He'll make all the major decisions and leave just the details to his subordinates."

"Why is that?" I wanted to know.

"Because Libras hate detail work. It bores them. LBJ, on the other hand, is a Virgo. He loves details."

"Does that mean Trudeau will be a good or a bad Prime Minister?"

"This coming year looks very good for him," mother revealed. "I'll tell you one thing: If something goes wrong, Trudeau won't pass the buck. He'll take the blame himself. Libras have a great sense of justice and fair play."

"Is he as confident as he looks?" I pried.

"No. If anything, Trudeau underestimates himself. He loves praise but it won't go to his head."

"That's a relief," I sighed.

"Trudeau isn't as down-to-earth as Mr. Pearson," mother advised.

"Why is that?"

"Mr. Pearson is Taurus. Libras have more charm, more flair. They're more artistic. More sensitive. But they are also more naive and less practical. Very idealistic."

"You mean. . . ."

"Libras are notorious for making bad first marriages. They'll send you roses but forget to bring home the groceries. Much better lovers than husbands, I'd say."

"Mother!"

"Trudeau may have all sorts of romances in this next year but nothing will come of them," she concluded.

"Whew! I'm glad to hear that. What about his political stance? Is he liberal or conservative?"

"That's hard to answer. What Trudeau believes today is not necessarily what he'll believe tomorrow. He'll discard an idea if he thinks he's found a better one."

"Tell that to the NDP," I suggested. "By the way, how is he with money?"

"Libras are funny about money. In some ways, they're cheap. They'll save on little things and then they'll go out and shoot the whole works on something very expensive—and never think about it."

"Could you give me a tip about Trudeau's religion?"

"Not very orthodox. He's a Catholic but I suspect even more— sort of a mystic, almost oriental. He's a mysterious man. That's Libra for you."

20

"Will he have a long career in Ottawa?" I begged.

"No. Not like Dief or Mackenzie King. To do the same thing for the next 15 or 20 years would bore him," mother said. "I'd give him 5 to 8 years in politics."

Eat your heart out, Peter Newman. She's MY mother.

July 18, 1968

This hide 'n' seek a two-way game

ONE OF THE "fun" things in Prime Minister Trudeau's life is playing hide'n'seek with the Canadian public.

He loves to pack a bag, buy an airline ticket for somewhere, and then dare the country to find him.

It's pretty jolly.

This past week, for example, Mr. Trudeau was hiding in Spain and other places too remote even to spell, let alone locate.

Before that, there was a weekend in the Laurentians. Or was it the mysterious trip "somewhere in the south" which turned out to be Florida?

In any case, he has become the Canadian equivalent of the Holy Grail, always being sought but never being found.

It's really a lot of fun.

The way it works is this:

Mr. Trudeau packs a few clean shirts, some socks and an RCMP inspector and then makes a dash for the airport of his choice.

Reporters in Ottawa count to 10 (with their eyes closed and leaning against a lamppost) and then begin looking for him.

The press loves the game.

A reporter can walk into his editor's office and say: "I have every reason to believe Mr. Trudeau is in Sydney, Australia. Could I have $5,000 in expense money to find him?"

The editor can't refuse.

In his mind, he sees the headline: "Evening News Reporter Locates Trudeau in Sydney, Australia."

All that for a measly $5,000. So he authorizes the expenses and the reporter is on his way.

The fact that Mr. Trudeau turns up in Three Rivers, Quebec, about two days later is incidental.

By then the reporter is basking on some Aussie beach, visiting his folks in Vancouver, or he's holed up in a downtown Toronto bar behind a table loaded with $5,000 worth of dry martinis.

The point is, he's been able to turn Mr. Trudeau's little game into a lovely holiday.

And he can always knock off a story that the PM was reported seen getting off a plane at the Hong Kong terminal if his paper wants copy.

Some critics claim this is a hell of a way to run a country. After all, MP is not supposed to stand for Marco Polo.

But Mr. Trudeau wants to play and he's the boss.

I've got my own plan.

Mr. Trudeau is a politician, right?

And politicians have to face elections every now and then.

Well, the next time there's an election, I'm going to hide and let Mr. Trudeau try to find me.

August 23, 1968

Bring back the days when great world simply ignored us

CANADA'S reputation is growing and a lot of us are worried. For years we rode at the back of the continent, known only for hockey, wheat and bad weather.

Our only national resource was Deanna Durbin. Our fashions were a safe 15 years behind Paris. And our speech was laughed at—especially when we said "about" and "khaki" and "house."

At best we were mistaken for Americans; and at worst we were confused for Nelson Eddy singing Rosemarie, I Love You.

In short, nobody paid very much attention to us.

And we were supremely happy.

22

No pressure. No prestige to worry about. No face that needed to be saved about 12 times a week in every corner of the world. No hate.

On the maps, we were content to be listed simply as "What's-their-name." Loved, respected and ignored—that was us.

But those blissful days are slipping away.

Reporters from all over the world are clamoring for interviews with Prime Minister Trudeau.

The Russians have finally condemned us at the United Nations. What's more, they even got our ambassador's name right.

God! Where did we go wrong?

And now, if that wasn't bad enough, Dick Gregory has predicted in an interview that Canada will emerge as the world's next great power.

God! Where did we go wrong?

Why pick on us? What have we ever done to Gregory to make him say something as rotten as that?

Why couldn't he have fingered the Swedes or the Mexicans or, to stretch a point, even the Australians?

Why do we have to be the ones to join the United States, Russia and China at the summit?

Who wants that Everest? No friends. A crisis every day. Constant criticism. The target of envy and lust.

No thanks!

Obviously, we've all got to pitch in before Canada gets kicked upstairs. And the place to start is at the top.

Here's my plan.

First, Prime Minister Trudeau tones down his wardrobe, cuts out the kissing and trades in his Mercedes for a Terraplane.

That would eliminate his (and our) status as swingers.

It would help, too, if he laced his conversation with a few "by gars" and even a couple of "sacre bleus" the next time he talks to the New York Times.

Next, we flood the world with post cards from beautiful Flin Flon and say the photograph on the front is actually Toronto, Canada's leading city.

Pow! There goes our reputation in the business community.

To eliminate our military prestige, we arrange for our troops to challenge the Liechtenstein army in a tug-of-war—and lose.

In a matter of weeks, we'll be reduced to second-class status again—and beautiful anonymity.

So let's get out there and lose.

Nobody can call us a "great power" and get away with it.

September 9, 1968

An inside look at Pierre

JUST A FEW days ago the furrier who designed Prime Minister Pierre Elliott Trudeau's otter coat gave an interview to the press.

Before that, we had a story from Mr. Trudeau's barber who described the PM's hair in detail for a breathless audience.

Obviously, it's only a matter of time before we turn on our television sets and hear something like this . . .

"Good evening, ladies and gentlemen. I'm Charles Templeton and tonight the CTV network is pleased to bring you an exclusive 90-minute feature on the Prime Minister's body.

"Right here, on our screen, you will see actual x-rays of Mr. Trudeau's liver—and in living color.

"You will meet the lab technician who took these x-rays and he will face a panel of newspapermen who will be free to ask any questions they wish about the liver.

"As well as this in-depth look at Mr. Trudeau's liver, we will show close-ups of the Prime Minister's elbow, his neck and, if time permits, his clavicle.

"But first we'd like you to meet Dr. D.D. Extractor, a dentist who has worked on Prime Minister Trudeau's teeth. Welcome, doctor."

"Good evening, Mr. Templeton."

"Dr. Extractor, could you give us a funny anecdote about Mr. Trudeau's teeth."

"There isn't much to tell, really. Mr. Trudeau's teeth speak for themselves."

"What about Mr. Trudeau's overbite, doctor? I understand that it's a well known fact in dental circles that he has an over-bite."

"That's true—but it's not serious."

"Could you draw Mr. Trudeau's over-bite on the blackboard

behind you and, while you're at it, tell our audience what the Prime Minister says while in your chair."

"Mostly just 'Aaaaaah!' You see, I've got my hand in his mouth and that makes it pretty difficult to speak."

"Could you hold up your hand, doctor, so our viewers can see the hand that's been in Prime Minister Trudeau's mouth? Yes—show your thumb, too. Do Mr. Trudeau's palms sweat during an extraction?"

"No more than normal."

"How about his wisdom teeth? Would you say there is anything distinctive about them?"

"No."

"You wouldn't happen to have a plastic model of his wisdom teeth, would you, doctor?"

"I did have one but I got the Prime Minister to autograph it and I gave it to my wife as a birthday gift."

"It would make a nice conversational piece. I see you've brought some things with you, doctor. Could you tell us what you have there?"

"Here's a 1957 copy of Liberty magazine which the Prime Minister read one day in my waiting room while waiting to have his gums checked.

"Here's some dental floss I used while checking over his teeth on his last appointment.

"And here's something I prize—an old filling which I took from one of his molars after he bit too hard on a piece of peanut brittle."

"Doctor, thank you for coming to the studio and giving us insight into Mr. Trudeau. I think we all know him a little better as a result."

"You're welcome, Mr. Templeton."

"Now stay with us, folks. We'll be back after station break with Mr. Trudeau's liver and other surprises. . . ."

September 12, 1968

PM gave de Gaulle a regular French dressing down

I HATE to be the one to say it but Prime Minister Trudeau has handled the current French crisis all wrong.

When he heard that the government of France was sending "spies" and "agents provocateur" to Canada, Mr. Trudeau blew his cool.

He told Charles de Gaulle (among other things) to keep his agitators to himself. It was a regular French dressing down.

However, instead of getting mad, our Prime Minister should get even.

Why not fight fire with fire.

My proposal is that we immediately send an agent provocateur to France and give de Gaulle some of his own medicine.

And I volunteer for the job.

When I arrive in Paris, I intend to go directly to the Ritz hotel with no fewer than 15 pieces of luggage and register as "Pierre Elliott Trudeau."

After the bellboy has carried my luggage to my room, opened the window, turned on the television and shown me the bathroom, I'll tip him the equivalent of 10 cents.

He'll fly into a rage, call me a lot of dirty names and rush down to the lobby to tell the other help that I'm a cheap swine.

It will probably mean a general strike.

That evening, according to my plan, I'll eat at Longchamps or, perhaps, Maxims.

When the waiter brings my coq au vin, I'll ask (in a loud voice) for the ketchup.

When the word gets to the kitchen, the chef will stuff his head inside an oven (a 500-degree oven for those of you taking this down) and light a match.

Pow! He'll go to pieces. Little ones.

Naturally, I intend to pay my check with a $20 Canadian bill, and when the waiter puts out his hand, I'll shake it.

From the restaurant, I'll hail a taxi to see what I can uncover at the Folies Bergere.

When the gorgeous star of the show comes on stage, completely nude, of course, I'll stand up and shout at her: "Boo! Bring on the girls!"

It could mean the end of sex as an industry in France.

But I won't stop there.

I'll walk into Dior's and ask to see something in a housedress size 44, for five or six bucks.

I'll say to cab drivers, "Nice little town you have here. Not exactly a Winnipeg, but nice."

I'll demand sliced bread, for heaven's sake.

In short, I'll bug the French. I'll provoke them. I'll have de Gaulle eating out of my hand in a week.

To get me out of Paris, de Gaulle will promise to recall all of his agents provocateur from Canada—and throw in Brigitte Bardot to sweeten the deal.

Now what could be simpler than that?

September 20, 1968

Please, Mr. Trudeau, don't go snooping into my sex life

PRIME MINISTER Trudeau has just about ruined me.

A few days ago he got mad at the press for snooping into his private life and suggested he might retaliate by giving us a dose of our own medicine.

The PM even hinted he would ask police to keep us under surveillance and to report back on our sex lives.

When I got the news, I immediately rushed home even though it was just the middle of the afternoon.

"What are you . . ." my wife began.

"Shut up and kiss me!" I demanded. "Not here in the hallway—in the living room, in front of the picture window, so everyone can see."

"Are you nuts?" she asked.

"Haven't you heard?" I whispered into her ear. "Trudeau's got

27

this house under 24-hour watch."

"So what?" my wife wanted to know.

"So how would it look if some Mountie goes back to Ottawa and hands Trudeau a dossier on my sex life with nothing in it?" I answered. "Would you mind biting my neck?"

"I don't see any Mountie watching the house," my wife commented as I nibbled on her ear.

"Tear off my shirt," I said.

"That shirt cost $6.95 on sale," my wife muttered. "I'm not tearing it for any Mountie. Besides, it won't tear."

"Try grabbing it at the collar," I begged. "Then just sort of yank. You know, the way they do in Italian movies."

"It still won't tear," my wife said. "It's guaranteed for a full year. I'd have to get scissors or a knife."

"Then muss my hair," I pleaded. "And please look as if you're enjoying it. My reputation is at stake."

"Is this all right?" my wife inquired.

"Perfect," I answered. "Do you think you could breathe hard for a minute or two?"

"This is stupid," she balked. "There's nobody watching the house. I'd have seen a Mountie if he was standing around outside."

"He may be disguised as a tree," I pointed out. "Kiss me again and this time throw in a hug. Look as if you're having fun."

"I don't have time for all this fooling around," my wife nagged. "Can I go back to the kitchen? I've got a meat loaf baking."

"Stop talking like a wife and throw me down on the chesterfield," I instructed. "The last thing I want is for Trudeau to think my sex life is dull."

"Won't I hurt your back if I throw you on the chesterfield?" my wife suggested. "You know how temperamental your back is."

"Maybe you're right," I agreed. "Better just blow in my ear and leave it at that."

"All right but that's it," my wife stated. "I've got supper to make."

Well, this has been going on for several days now. Every time I go near a window I kiss my wife, hug my wife, sweep her into my arms.

I hope those Mounties get their damned report into Trudeau soon.

28

I don't know how much more of this sort of thing my marriage can take.

January 21, 1969

Gord Sinclair could be balance to Pope

PRIME MINISTER Trudeau stirred up a hornet's nest last week when he suggested Canada may send an ambassador to the Vatican.

Cries of protest have come from all quarters but chiefly from citizens who believe in the traditional separation of church and state.

They feel it's unfair to single out the Roman Catholic Church for this special honor.

Naturally, the cabinet's been concerned.

Over the weekend they met in emergency session in Ottawa to see what they can do to soothe the feelings of non-Catholics.

After going over the statistics, the government learned that millions of Canadians don't go to any church on the average Sunday morning, especially during golf season.

Therefore, they think they've come up with the perfect compromise.

When Trudeau sends an ambassador to the Vatican he will also extend full diplomatic recognition to Gordon Sinclair.

That way agnostics and atheists in Canada won't feel slighted.

If they have a direct line to Ottawa, too, they aren't liable to be bitter over any little favor given to the Catholics.

In its present form, the plan will work this way:

The few square blocks surrounding Gordon Sinclair's home in Metro Toronto will be declared unsanctified ground and Mr. Sinclair will be invited to set up his own state.

If Mr. Sinclair wants to print his own stamps, set up his own souvenir shops and even establish a guard in colorful uniforms to stand outside his home, that will be up to him.

29

The important thing is that agnostics and atheists will at last have a non-spiritual home.

All religious activity will be outlawed in Mr. Sinclair's sectless see—prayer, hymns, bingo, Girl Guide cookies, raffles, potluck suppers and open-line radio programs.

That way one disbelief won't be favored over another.

At present there are all sorts of religious lobbies operating in Ottawa—Catholic lobbies, Jewish lobbies, United Church lobbies, Anglican lobbies, Seventh Day Adventist lobbies.

But doubters and sceptics have no official voice in the nation's capital and have to rely on an occasional plug from Pierre Berton or Bishop Pike.

Recognition of Mr. Sinclair would solve that problem as well as balance out the offer to the Vatican.

There are other advantages, too.

By giving Mr. Sinclair his independence and maintaining an envoy in his home, Ottawa would gain a valuable listening post.

Besides, it never hurts to establish diplomatic relations with a state that can lend you a few million till payday.

Gordon Sinclair would make a perfect country.

January 22, 1969

Chapter 2: Enigma

Trudeau, reporters hoping for peace

AS EVERY Canadian knows, the Prime Minister and the press have been waging an undeclared war ever since the commonwealth conference in London.

Fortunately, I was able to secure an exclusive interview yesterday with a journalist who has just returned from the front in Ottawa.

"What's it like up there?" I asked.

"Nasty," he said. "You can't raise your head without an innuendo whistling by your ear or an accusation exploding in your face."

"Have you suffered any injuries yourself?"

"Yes—three cold shoulders, one piercing stare and at least a dozen mutters."

"What do you mean by a mutter?"

"It's one of the PM's favorite weapons. He starts to mutter or even mumble when he's giving a speech to throw you off. It really messes up your notes."

"I thought this war would be fought according to the rules of the Geneva convention," I stated.

"Anything goes," the vet revealed. "Just the other day I was at a government press reception and I got an hors d'oeuvre with a toothpick lodged inside."

"You mean . . ."

"It was no accident. Not only that, all they served was soft drinks."

"I didn't realize there was such hatred on both sides," I confessed. "Is there any chance of arranging a ceasefire?"

"The hawks in the press gallery don't want a ceasefire," he explained. "They want to fight right down to the wire, to escalate and flood Ottawa with so many reporters that the PM will surrender unconditionally."

I asked about his own feelings.

"I think we should sit down and reason together," he admitted. "You might say I'm dovish."

"Funny, you don't look dovish," I commented.

"Unfortunately," he continued, "we can't decide on the shape of the table to be used in any peace talks. The PM wants a rectangular table with his cabinet on one side and the Ottawa political analysts on the other."

"Isn't that acceptable?"

"No. We want a round table and equal representation for cartoonists, editorial writers, rewrite men and columnists from across the country."

"That seems fair," I agreed.

"We also want the Prime Minister to promise not to take any unfair advantage if a ceasefire is arranged."

"What do you mean?"

"We'll call off our photographers and legmen provided Mr. Trudeau agrees not to have any dates during the negotiations period."

"Is he agreeable?"

"He wants to compromise—no dates with redheads or brunettes during the ceasefire, only blondes."

"You give a little and you get a little," I sighed. "By the way, why are you in town?"

"To pick up supplies—some typewriter ribbons, copy paper and a few pencils," he answered. "Besides, I'm supposed to phone Bob Hope. We want him to do his TV show from the press gallery next Christmas."

January 24, 1969

Our love turns to war as PM's charisma curdles

I'VE BEEN afraid of this—the "hawks" in the press gallery have won out.

Our war against Prime Minister Trudeau is being escalated in Ottawa and it's going to be nasty.

When the tension in Canada's mid-east began to mount almost a year ago, I pleaded for restraint on both sides.

As a "dove," I suggested the Prime Minister might have a good reason for giving us the slip and taking off on holidays without us.

Some reporters said I was nuts.

They're the ones who embrace the "domino" theory which maintains that if we lose the Prime Minister as a "contact" in Ottawa, it won't be long before every cabinet minister, every civil servant, is thumbing his nose at us.

"I say we make a stand," one veteran columnist stated. "Let's get in there and let our typewriters speak for us."

If you'll recall, after that, new, more critical headlines began appearing in the newspaper—Prime Minister Trudeau Goofs Grey Cup Kickoff and Prime Minister Trudeau Wears a Fur Coat.

Mr. Trudeau counter-attacked with an occasional icy stare and a barrage of "no comment."

When "charisma" became "enigma" in the press, even a fool could see what was ahead.

Newspapers began pouring war material into the capital—more copy paper, more ballpoint pens, more sophisticated taping devices.

Editors and publishers began infiltrating the House of Commons in the guise of "observers" and interviews were sought with some of the Prime Minister's lady friends.

I begged that we sit down and reason together but nobody would listen.

Prime Minister Trudeau let fly a telling blow in London by referring to reporters as "creeps."

The press retaliated by referring to him as being in his 50th year, rather than as 49.

A girl was located who agreed to testify that the Prime Minister didn't kiss as well as her boyfriend.

The PM sniffed he didn't read newspapers.

In spite of that sadistic shot, some of us were still hopeful we could get together on neutral ground and negotiate a ceasefire.

We were even willing to go to Hull and back if it meant a pause in the insults.

And, I can tell you now, we were prepared to withdraw a research assistant, three copy girls and a detachment of our best rewrite men from the Ottawa front to show our good intentions.

All we sought in return was recognition of the press at public meetings.

Instead, Prime Minister Trudeau held more secret talks last week and told reporters to "go home and have a bath."

That's when we pushed The Button.

We brought out our best photographers, stationed them in rafters, and ordered them to take pictures of the bald spot on top of Prime Minister Trudeau's head.

You probably saw them in the paper.

If that doesn't bring him to his knees, I don't know what will.

June 18, 1969

How Pierre can prove he means economy

PRIME MINISTER Trudeau has had more than his share of bad moments this week.

He's been roughed up by pacifists who threatened to tear him limb from limb if he didn't put a stop to the awful violence in the world.

The Indians (only 9 per cent of whom have indoor plumbing) have accused him of wanting to change their way of life.

When he closed off debate in Parliament, the newspapers called him "arrogant"; when he tried to explain his point of view to street demonstrators in Vancouver, the same writers complained he was "undignified."

The PM just can't win.

And now, to make things worse, Trudeau is on an economy wave and intends to give taxpayers a break by cutting government expenditures.

Stanley Knowles of the NDP is already hopping mad and has attacked the prime minister for "turning back the clock."

Obviously, Trudeau has no alternative—he'll have to cut his personal expenses, too, in order to prove he's sincere.

That's not easy for a bachelor.

However, if the Prime Minister wants to turn off the critics, these are just some of the promises he may have to make to the Canadian public:

To use regular gasoline in his Mercedes sports car rather than hi-test octanes—and to fill up at service stations where they give away dinnerware.

To accept at least three dinner invitations each week from mothers of unwed daughters, thus cutting the food budget at 24 Sussex Drive by almost half.

To buy a plastic carnation for his buttonhole which can be dry cleaned and used over and over again.

To make it clear to all girl friends that it will be Dutch treat when they go out on dates—and definitely no shrimp cocktail from the a la carte menu.

To use only a domestic after-shave lotion, except on weekends.

To say he's married when he buys his airline tickets so that he and his staff can travel "family plan."

To ask beautiful women to bring their own paper cups if they want to sip champagne at some midnight tete-a-tete.

To hollanderize his fur coat and "make do" for another season.

To date only girls with rich fathers so that the country won't get stuck with the caterer's bill if the PM ever decides to settle down.

To join a helicopter pool to cut transportation costs this skiing season.

To buy only drip-dry monograms for his smoking jackets.

And, finally, to use margarine instead of the "high-cost" spread when buttering up the public.

Surely Stanley Knowles will accept that.

August 14, 1969

36

They shouldn't turn
Pierre Trudeau loose
on a powerless mob

PRIME MINISTER Trudeau announced this week that he's still willing to plunge into any crowd to discuss the issues of our time.

However, the real question is whether any crowd in Canada is willing to mingle with the PM.

Only a couple of weeks ago, a Vancouver crowd challenged Trudeau to a debate and, after the dust had cleared, it turned out the crowd had come out second best.

The Prime Minister hadn't even bruised his carnation.

But all sorts of people in the crowd showed up the next day with welts, scrapes and bumps which they claimed they had suffered at the hands of the Prime Minister.

Naturally, a crowd is going to think twice before it ever takes Trudeau on again.

My own feeling is that I would be willing to be part of a crowd discussing the issues with the Prime Minister—but only if he will agree to certain conditions.

For example, I'd want a guarantee that police will provide adequate protection for the crowd in case Trudeau gets angry and decides to mug us.

I'd also want the Prime Minister's word that he won't attack any crowd numbering fewer than 500.

All rabbit punches should be banned.

And the same goes for biting, eye-gouging and hitting below the belt.

That brings up the matter of Trudeau's hands.

As everybody knows, the PM is a karate expert and it isn't fair to let him loose against a crowd with that kind of advantage.

We wouldn't have a chance.

Therefore, I think he should agree in the future to make all of his speeches with one hand tied behind his back, at least during the question-and-answer period.

It would be even more comforting if the PM would disarm his hands before every public meeting by bathing them in Lux soap.

No defenceless crowd should be asked to face a man who splits pine boards with his fingertips and has a complete range of Oriental grunts at his command.

The very least we need is a barbed wire barricade which the Prime Minister can't jump if he gets unruly and out of hand.

If Trudeau agrees to de-escalate his strike power, he may be able to scrape up enough people to form a crowd for his next open debate.

Who knows, he might even entice some of those Vancouver hippies back for a second round, once they heal up.

If they're smart, though, they'll stay down at the waterfront, where it's safe.

August 29, 1969

"Great to be back eh, Mr. Trudeau"

PRIME MINISTER Pierre Elliott Trudeau has climbed mountains, faced angry mobs, challenged the raging seas and fought powerful men.

But I'd like to know how he stands up to something really tough that first day back at the office.

After a three-week holiday in the Mediterranean, Trudeau reported back on the job Wednesday and it's my guess the conversation went like this . . .

"Good morning, Mr. Trudeau," an aide probably greeted.

"What's so good about it?" the Prime Minister undoubtedly wanted to know.

"Well . . . oh, I understand, sir. First day back and all of that. Never mind. We'll get right at it and . . .

"My collar's killing me. Whoever invented the necktie and starched collar should be taken out and hung from the nearest tree."

"I'll make a note of it, sir. Now about Quebec and . . ."

"To hell with Quebec. Did I tell you about the fish I almost caught off the coast of Greece? She was three feet long if she was an inch. What a beauty!"

"Of course, sir."

"I just hope my pictures turn out. I got some snaps of Capri that you wouldn't believe."

"Could we get back to Quebec and the French-English problem, sir?"

"I don't feel like solving the French-English problem right now. Why don't we send out for coffee and a Danish?"

"Very well, sir, but the work has rather piled up."

"Did anybody call while I was away?"

"Yes, sir. President Nixon, Prime Minister Wilson, the foreign minister for Red China, Queen . . ."

"Say, did I tell you about the little restaurant we found on Majorca? You'll love it—checkered table cloths, fantastic food and a guitar player who could make a stone cry."

"I'm sure it's very nice, sir. Now about the phone calls. You have a list there of 268 calls you're supposed to return some time today. And there's the mail—14,789 letters which . . ."

"Did you get the post card I sent from Nice? What a place! I didn't see a cloud in the sky for five days straight."

"I hate to interrupt, sir, but there are delegations waiting in the hall from the Indians, the labor movement, the poor, the consumers, the Eskimos, the . . ."

"Did I mention we got nearly seven miles per gallon on the yacht? That's not bad. And you've never seen a sunset until you've seen a Mediterranean sunset from the deck of a yacht."

"But, sir, Mr. Marchand wants a few words with you, there's a report on inflation on your desk, we have an urgent call re the crisis in the Middle East . . ."

"What time is it now?"

"Just seven minutes past nine o'clock, sir."

"My God! Will this day ever end?"

September 12, 1969

Chapter 3: The Swinger

Barbra breaks news to Momma

THANKS to the miracle of modern science, we switch you to a kitchen somewhere in the United States...

"Momma, there's something I want to tell you."

"What is it, Barbra?"

"Momma, there's this fella I've met and, well, I think we're getting serious."

"That's nice, Barbra. It's time you settled down, got a nice home in the suburbs, raised some children. What's this fella's name?"

"Pierre."

"Pierre? What kind of a name is that?"

"It's French."

"French? What's the matter, isn't Brooklyn good enough for you any more? You become a big shot movie star and all of a sudden you've got a French fella. So you want to break your father's heart?"

"But he's a very nice fella, Momma. Honest."

"What does this very nice French fella do for a living? Is he a doctor?"

"No."

"Maybe he's an accountant like your cousin Murray? Accountants make very good husbands. Besides, they don't work weekends and can afford live-in help."

"No, he's not an accountant."

"Does he run a little store somewhere? Or a delicatessen? Your father wouldn't mind a French fella if he was in cold cuts."

"Momma, Pierre runs a country—Canada. It's north of here."

"Canada, shmanada. Who needs it? Sadie-next-door's daughter married a man in dry goods. She gets everything 50 per cent off. Who wants snow wholesale?"

"But...."

"So what do I say when I meet Sadie on the street? 'My daughter Barbra's marrying a man from Canada and he can get me chilblains at cost.' Is that what I say?"

"Pierre is very important, Momma."

"If he's so important, maybe he could introduce you to a nice engineer, maybe somebody who builds bridges or apartment blocks."

"But I think I'm in love with Pierre."

"How old is this Pierre person?"

"He's 50."

"Are you crazy? That's almost as old as your father and God forbid you should marry somebody like that. You don't know what it's like to have a husband who . . . "

"Momma, Pierre is young for his age. He skis and swims and jogs."

"Barbra, marriage is more than skiing and swimming and jogging. Believe me, get a nice young doctor from the United States and I can die happy."

"I'm sorry, Momma, but Pierre gave me the flower from his button hole and . . . "

"A flower in his button hole! A 50-year-old Frenchman from Canada who doesn't even have his own business! Why don't you just take out a big butcher knife and kill me?"

"Momma, you'll like him if you just give him a chance. I want you to meet him. Could I invite him down for the weekend?"

"All right. I don't make any promises—but invite him down. He may not be what we wanted for you but as long as he's Jewish . . . "

"That's another thing, Momma. Momma? Speak to me, Momma! Momma . . . "

February 4, 1970

Ever wonder why PM's dates are always knockouts?

HAVE YOU EVER wondered why Prime Minister Trudeau is never caught in a clinch with a homely girl?

They may be blonde or brunette, French or English, from the

east coast or the west, Jewish or Catholic—but they're always knockouts.

For a long time I've suspected that the PM's knack for running into beautiful women was more than luck.

And, as it's turned out, I'm right.

By pulling strings, I've been able to interview the Mountie who is in charge of the Prime Minister's kissing detail.

On the guarantee that I would keep his identity secret, he held nothing back.

"I assume you're Mr. Trudeau's bodyguard," I began.

"No," he said. "I'm listed in the official record as a lipguard."

"Could you explain what a lipguard does?"

"Simply, it's my job to make sure the Prime Minister isn't the target of any unwanted kisses."

"How do you do that?"

"When the PM makes a public appearance, I check the crowd for thick ankles, unattractive busts and dangerous overbites."

"If I spot a steno with a handlebar moustache, for example, or a piece of spinach caught between her teeth, I steer the Prime Minister the other way—usually into the arms of somebody built like Raquel Welch."

"I've seen the results of your work and permit me to say you've got very good taste when it comes to hugging and squeezing."

"Thank you. In the osculation division of the force, our motto is, 'We always get our woman.'"

"Do plain girls ever persist in their attempt to corner the Prime Minister?"

"Occasionally. Fortunately, you can't kiss what you can't reach and all they usually get for their efforts is an epaulette in the mouth or a jab with a badge.

"However, we do run into really stubborn cases which we call the kamikaze kissers—the women who are determined to steal a kiss or die in the attempt."

"What steps do you take then?"

"Very fast ones. We try to outrun the suspect, if possible.

"And, if that doesn't work, it's up to me to make the supreme sacrifice."

"You mean . . ."

"As a woman makes a lunge for the Prime Minister, I throw my lips in the way and intercept the pucker."

"Well, at least the work isn't as dangerous as the Musical Ride or highway patrol," I consoled.

"That's what you think," he answered. "I was at an Eskimo reception with the PM last year and broke my nose in two places in the line of duty."

February 24, 1970

PM could be part-time postie on world travels

PRIME MINISTER Pierre Trudeau said recently he plans to take matters into his own hands if Canada's postal strike isn't settled soon.

To get more information on this intriguing development, I called the man who sees Mr. Trudeau more often than anybody— his travel agent.

"How is the PM?" I began.

"Wonderful," the agent replied. "He's enjoying the Mediterranean sunshine after his Caribbean holiday and he sends his best to you and the other people in Canada."

"Could you tell me the purpose of this vacation?"

"It's twofold. First, Mr. Trudeau wanted to see for himself how Canada's war against inflation is going."

"And?"

"The Prime Minister is happy with what he's found. There are fewer Canadians staying at luxury hotels on the continent right now than there were in December when Mr. Trudeau made his last check."

"That is a good sign," I agreed.

"After all this talk about austerity, Mr. Trudeau would have been heartbroken if he had discovered the Mediterranean beaches swarming with Canadians," the agent admitted.

"But, as far as he can tell, he is the only Canadian who has had a holiday in both the Mediterranean and the Caribbean within the past two weeks.

"It means the restraints he suggested for the country are working."

"According to the papers, the Prime Minister is also planning to visit Moscow and Singapore this year," I mentioned.

"That's right," the travel agent said proudly. "As close as we can figure, he'll have travelled to six continents before the year is out."

"But what about the mail strike?" I interrupted, getting to the matter at hand. "How does he plan to handle that?"

"That's the second reason for the current vacation," came the reply.

"Do you recall the Prime Minister stating he would personally intervene if the strike dragged on much longer?"

I said I did.

"What Mr. Trudeau intends to do if the post office and the government can't come to terms soon is deliver the mail personally.

"He has been busy setting up depots around the world since the beginning of the year.

"With luck, the PM feels he can take vacations in 80 or 90 countries each year—and take a bag of mail with him on every trip.

"That way Canadians with friends in Rome or Sydney or Hong Kong or Honolulu or the Riviera will still have mail service."

"What about mail delivery inside the country?" I asked.

"Mr. Trudeau is hoping to visit Canada once a year, too," the agent confided.

August 27, 1970

Iron bars do not a prison make Quebeckers find

QUEBEC LABOR LEADER Michel Chartrand delivered a three-minute address to a union meeting on Monday.

45

And what made the speech especially interesting was the fact that Mr. Chartrand was behind bars in a Montreal jail at the time.

Fortunately, the talk was made on tape, not in person.

However, as you can imagine, there were a lot of red faces when the news got out.

Nobody was more embarrassed than the critics of the War Measures Act who claim Prime Minister Trudeau has turned Canada into a police state and taken away our freedom of speech.

Obviously, if a man in solitary confinement can still speak his mind, the rest of us don't have much to worry about.

"It wouldn't have been so bad if Mr. Chartrand had recorded his speech several months ago," a spokesman for the anti-War Measures group complained.

"But it was obviously taped in his cell earlier that same day."

"We can hardly charge the government with keeping political prisoners incommunicado if the political prisoners won't co-operate by keeping their mouths shut."

"Couldn't you hint the speech is a fraud, something pieced together from old talks delivered by Mr. Chartrand in pre-War Measures Act days?" I suggested.

"We thought of that but everybody, including the police, is convinced it's genuine.

"Besides, Robert Lemieux delivered a speech from his cell in solitary confinement on the same day.

"Frankly, we're discouraged.

"We'll never get the War Measures Act repealed as long as Chartrand and Lemieux insist on accepting speaking engagements while in maximum security."

"You'll just have to keep plugging away," I consoled.

"It isn't easy," my contact whimpered. "Speeches from jail, letters smuggled to the Quebec Bar Association, suspects escaping from secret compartments in walls.

"Sometimes I think we'll never prove Canada has become a police state.

"You don't suppose the police are deliberately trying to make us look bad, do you?"

"I prefer to think it's just a coincidence," I said.

November 20, 1970

46

"I didn't raise a son of mine to hang around Parliament"

I CALLED my mother on the telephone yesterday to give her the good news.

"The paper wants to send me to Ottawa to cover Parliament for a few days," I said. "Isn't that wonderful?"

There was dead silence.

"Do you hear me, Mom? I said the paper wants . . ."

"I heard you," mother interrupted. "And you can't go."

"What do you mean I can't go?"

"I mean I didn't raise a son of mine to hang around Parliament."

"But . . ."

"No buts. I've heard the kind of language the Prime Minister uses and I don't want you around that kind of talk. You're only 42."

"Mom, George Bain, Charlie Lynch and Anthony Westell are with the Prime Minister all the time for stories."

"That's their mothers' problems, not mine. How do you think I'd feel, sitting at home, wondering if you were at a press conference with Mr. Trudeau?

"For all I know, he might even give you an exclusive interview—and how would I explain that to your Aunt Nellie?"

"I promise I won't hang around the Prime Minister."

"Sure, that's easy to say—now.

"But you'll be in the press gallery some day and a smart aleck reporter will suggest, 'Let's talk to the Prime Minister.'

"Rather than be a spoilsport, you'll go along and there you'll be, taking down four-letter words like the rest of them."

"Just because a reporter uses a swear word in a quote doesn't mean he approves of it," I pointed out.

"A boy is known by the company he keeps," mother maintained. "The way Parliament is carrying on, Hansard may soon come out with a centerfold."

"If I go to Ottawa, I promise I won't spell out everything the Prime Minister says. I'll just write h . . . and d . . . and f . . ."

"Your editor will probably fill in the blanks and we're back where we started.

"Besides, you wouldn't do a good job in Ottawa. You haven't described an obscene gesture since you were a sports writer, eight years ago.

"You're probably rusty."

"All right, I won't go to Ottawa," I surrendered.

"Good," mother said. "Maybe I'll let you interview the Prime Minister later, when he grows up."

February 19, 1971

I have some words Trudeau could use...

PRIME MINISTER Trudeau's language of command has become front page news again.

He's the only politician in Canada who can clear his throat, and the hall, at the same time.

That's because, when angered, the PM resorts to some pretty earthy phrases.

In fact, if there were a college specializing in words, our leader would be a four-letter man.

Or, to put it another way, Mr. Trudeau is the kind of person who wouldn't say shoot if he had a mouthful.

Frankly, its understandable.

Answering dozens of questions every day about high taxes, high unemployment and hijinks must be unnerving.

However, many people are getting nervous about the lip service the Prime Minister pays them.

They're not sure what he's going to say next, let alone last.

As a result, I've prepared a little speech which the PM can use the next time he's in a tight corner and wants to put some snotty MP in his place—and not shock the citizenry.

"Golly gee whiz (he can begin) I realize unemployment is too gosh dang high in this darn country.

"Any son of a bee's wax knows that.

48

"But can't you donkeys see that you don't just turn off a recession overnight?

"Jumpin' Jehosaphat, I'm working my ears off and all you beggars do is sit back and fuddle duddle me.

"Well, I've had it.

"You can eat worms for all I care, or take a running jump.

"I'm in charge and if you don't like it, lump it, put it in your pipe and smoke it, or go to Halifax and back.

"You're darn tootin' we've got economic problems. But, holy kimollee, they're not going to be solved by some mother on the Opposition bench calling me names.

"I'll be a son of a sea cook before I'll let you get away with that.

"Whilikers, you mischievous imps don't seem to give a hang or a rip about my feelings.

"If that's the way you want it, suck eggs. I've taken enough of your sassafras.

"As far as I'm concerned, you're full of horse feathers—and so's your old man.

"Criminy!"

If I do say so myself, it's the best damn speech I ever wrote for the PM.

February 23, 1971

Chapter 4: Domesticity

"Okay, buttercup, but don't you tell Uncle Edgar"

AFTER every honeymoon there comes that moment of truth when the bride cuddles up in her husband's arms and whispers, "I'll need some housekeeping money."

How will our Prime Minister, a newlywed at 51, handle that domestic issue with his bride of 22?

Perhaps the conversation will go like this . . .

"How much will you need, my queen of hearts?"

"Golly, $175 a week should be about right, my Gallic god. That would take care of the groceries, my ballet lesson, and my membership in the Wayne Newton record-of-the-month club."

"My precious buttercup, I'd like nothing better than to give you $175 to run the house—but it wouldn't be in the best interests of the country."

"Why not, my Galahad?"

"Because it would be inflationary, O beauty worthy of a maharajah's ransom. An allowance of $175 a week would put too much pressure on the economy."

"But if I spent $175 a week, wouldn't it help stimulate the cash flow at the supermarket and improve the economy, star without equal in the heaven of my love?"

"On the contrary, delicious lady, it would push prices even higher, create more demand for checkout clerks—and weaken our battle against inflation."

"How much do you think my allowance should be, my charismatic Cupid?"

"Thirty-five dollars a week, my pet."

"But I don't think I can manage on $35 a week, gold nugget in the mountain stream of my very existence. Besides, there'll soon be another mouth to feed."

"You mean . . ."

"Yes, our live-in Mountie, I hope you haven't forgotten him, sugar pie."

"When you smile at me, I succumb, enchantress of ten thousand delights. All right—$50 a week, but don't tell the finance minister how we're throwing it around."

"That's still pretty skimpy, my adorable Adonis. What happens if you bring a king home for lunch? On $50 a week, I can't serve steak."

"Why not, invaluable diamond in the tiara of my soul?"

"Because filet is $3.50 a pound, O Shakespeare of hugs and kisses."

"That's awful, unreachable star in the firmament of beauty. How can married people afford it?"

"They can't unless they get more money, my black belt in the karate of love. So you have a choice—you can either eat, or fight inflation."

"Very well—you can have $175 a week to run the house, fairest in all the land. But we won't be able to send you to camp this summer."

March 10, 1971

Trudeau must stop this peace-making

PRIME MINISTER Trudeau has done it again. Goofed.

He's just signed a peace pact in Moscow with Premier Kosygin.

By terms of the agreement, Canada and Russia have agreed to shake hands and not come out fighting.

In addition, the two nations plan to sit down and discuss mutual problems.

It's madness.

Of course it's wonderful to have friends in Moscow—halfway round the world.

But what about Washington?

There are people in high places in America's capital who consider a peace pact with Russia tantamount to a declaration of war.

They are not going to take our act of friendship lying down.

It wouldn't surprise me one bit if Spiro Agnew accused us of endangering world peace with our blatant display of pacifism.

This is non-violence at its very worst.

Mark my words, we'll pay for it.

Just a few days ago, a United States coast guard ship uncovered a deck cannon and threatened to fire on a Canadian fishing boat in our own waters.

And that was BEFORE Trudeau provocatively made his stand for peace in our hemisphere.

God only knows what would have happened if the skipper of the coast guard cutter had realized our PM was in Russia at the very moment trying to patch up world differences.

If Trudeau has any sense of decency and self preservation, he'll renounce the peace treaty with Moscow when he gets home.

As well, the Canadian ambassador in Washington should rush to the White House and make a formal apology for our PM's reckless bid for global harmony.

Trudeau should realize he can't go around spreading cool logic and warm handshakes when Mr. Nixon's back is turned.

After all, Mr. Nixon doesn't make trouble by sending a good-will mission to Quebec, does he?

May 24, 1971

The cabinet will help Pierre pick a name

PRIME MINISTER Pierre Trudeau called a special cabinet meeting a few days ago and made this announcement to his colleagues:

"Gentlemen, I want you to be the first to know that I decided to have a son."

There was applause.

"Yes, I'm planning to have a son and he'll be born later this year—in December.

"And the reason I've called you together is to help me pick a name."

Health Minister John Munro was the first to speak.

"Why not call your son John? John is a good solid name. It was the name of Canada's first prime minister and it would have an appeal for voters in my constituency."

"No. John has a Conservative ring to it. There's John Diefenbaker, John Robarts and, as you mentioned, Sir John A. Macdonald," Trudeau pointed out.

"John is not an appropriate name for a son of mine."

Finance Minister Edgar Benson was next.

"How about Ian? Ian is an economical name. It has a feeling of thrift about it. Besides, it would cost next to nothing to have Ian engraved on a comb and brush set."

"Ian is too Anglo-Saxon," Trudeau stated. "With an election coming up, perhaps next year, we have to think of these things.

"I'm afraid Ian is not an appropriate name for a son of mine."

"Would you consider something like Louis?" External Affairs Minister Mitchell Sharp inquired.

"In Quebec you could pronounce it Lou-ee and in Ontario you could say Lou-is. To older voters you could suggest the baby was named after Louis St. Laurent and to young voters you could hint you have Louis Riel in mind.

"Thanks to Joe Louis, Louis Quatorze, John L. Lewis, and a dance hall gal named Lou, Louis is a name for every one, regardless of background or sex."

"Louis has advantages," the PM agreed. "But it still isn't exactly what I had in mind."

The cabinet members began reeling off names starting with Adam and running through the alphabet, letter by letter.

Four hours later they still hadn't come up with a name the Prime Minister would accept.

Each time they had a suggestion, the PM would reject it, stating, "it isn't appropriate as a name for a son of mine."

Finally, Jean Marchand exploded.

"Holy Moses, we've . . ."

"Moses? Moses!" the PM interrupted. "No, but you're on the right track."

July 28, 1971

The scoop that made Viet Nam leak seem kindergarten stuff

IT'S EVERY reporter's dream to gain access to top-level government secrets and score a scoop.

So you can imagine how excited I was when an Ottawa contact telephoned yesterday and offered me the story of the year.

"This is hush-hush stuff," he whispered. "And it's yours exclusively—if you can come up with $5,000 in small, unmarked bills."

"Wow— $5,000 is a lot of money," I pointed out.

"This is a lot of story," my source guaranteed. "What I have makes the Viet Nam papers look like kindergarten stuff."

"You're kidding!"

"I don't kid for $5,000. George Bain, Charlie Lynch and that gang would give their right arm for this information."

"Is it that big?" I gasped.

"Just the biggest story in the country. I'm really going out on the limb to give it to you."

"I know—you've stumbled on the complete list of RCMP underground agents from coast to coast!"

"Bigger," my caller corrected.

"Don't tell me you've got your hands on Canada's defence plan in the event of a sneak atomic attack delivered by an unnamed superpower to the East! I'll buy it!"

"Can't you get your mind off piddling items and think big?" my caller asked, more than a trace of annoyance showing in his voice.

"There's only one story bigger than that...but it's impossible...nobody has that information...nobody!"

"Wrong. I have. I've got all the details of the Trudeau pregnancy—decorator plans for the nursery at 24 Sussex, artist sketches of the layette, dates of all the surprise baby showers, the phone number of the diaper service Mrs. Trudeau intends to use, data on the burping technique to be employed by the PM.

"I've even got the Prime Minister's exact words when he

learned he was going to be a father—and it's all yours for $5,000."

I was aghast.

"Do you realize the enormity of what you're doing?" I demanded. "Selling cabinet secrets is one thing—after all, everybody has to make a living.

"But peddling pre-natal information is hitting below the belt.

"The Prime Minister personally ordered a news blackout on the baby. He won't even tell Mrs. Trudeau the exact date she's expecting. And you come along and want to break security for money.

"It's despicable," I said, slamming down the phone.

In time, some news about the Trudeau baby may leak out—but it won't be my fault.

Thank God some of us in the newspaper game still put the safety of the country ahead of scoops.

August 3, 1971

Trudeau's straight-arm to wife's admirer not fair

ALL CANADIANS with a sense of fair play were dismayed to see newspaper photographs of Prime Minister Trudeau pushing aside some enthusiastic Maritimer in the process of stealing a kiss from Mrs. Trudeau.

What way is that for Mr. Trudeau to act?

When the Prime Minister was single, he went around the country kissing everybody else's wife.

Grit or Tory, rich or poor, French or English, teenage or in her early 20s, our Don Juanish leader kissed them all.

His lip stretched from sea to sea.

But now that he's got a wife of his own, apparently Mr. Trudeau wants to call off the game. He intends to turn on the lights and go home.

Well, what about the husbands in this country?

Statistics indicate the PM kissed 923,977 married women from the time he took office until his marriage earlier this year.

Whether you consider kissing a political or personal act, that still adds up to 923,977 kisses he owes.

And yet when one brave husband tried to reduce the debt by one, instead of a smack on the lips from Margaret all he got was a shove on the shoulder from Pierre.

Obviously, Mr. Trudeau considers kissing a one-way street.

When he had nothing to contribute to the national love-in but his own pucker, our Prime Minister was a swashbuckling romantic, the biggest hugger of them all.

However, now the bedroom slipper is on the other foot. It's goodbye Errol Flynn, hello Dagwood Bumstead.

Part of the problem, of course, is Mrs. Trudeau.

If she didn't happen to be so darn attractive, Mr. Trudeau probably wouldn't mind strangers stepping up and pecking at her cheek.

Being 923,977 kisses in arrears, he might even have encouraged his wife to open a booth at the CNE or Man and His World to settle his debts—if she looked like Phyllis Diller.

But there she is, a knockout.

Like every man with a gorgeous wife, Mr. Trudeau has adopted a hands-off policy on the domestic front and is not prepared to share his good fortune with the husband-on-the-street. And the 923,977 kisses he owes?

I'm afraid we'll just have to put that down to experience. His.

August 13, 1971

Some basic things to help change that playboy image

THE BEST BRAINS in the Liberal party have been busy all week.

Their problem: To de-glamorize Prime Minister Trudeau.

For years the PM has had a "playboy" image.

However, Senator Richard Stanbury told a Vancouver audience

it's time the party stressed the more serious side of its leader.

Unfortunately, it isn't easy changing images in mid-term.

However, here are just a few of the promises the Liberals want Mr. Trudeau to make.

That...

Mr. Trudeau will give up skiing this winter and join a bowling league in Hamilton.

Mr. Trudeau will get the name of Robert Stanfield's hair stylist.

Mr. Trudeau will fly economy to the next Commonwealth conference—unless a seat becomes available on a British Airways Show Tour charter.

Mr. Trudeau will keep last year's scuba suit and have his flippers half-soled in the interest of economy.

Mr. Trudeau will host a Paw Kettle film festival in Ottawa early in the new year.

Mr. Trudeau will have a pay phone installed in the back seat of his official car.

Mr. Trudeau will get Col. Saunders to cater the next government reception at 24 Sussex.

Mr. Trudeau will refuse to kiss anyone at his next public appearance who isn't over 65 years of age, plain and wearing Dr. Scholl wedgies.

Mr. Trudeau will order his next cravat (domestic) from Eaton's catalogue.

Mr. Trudeau will try to develop an ulcer before going to the country in a general election.

Mr. Trudeau will have his fur coat made into a scatter rug for the new nursery.

Mr. Trudeau will plan a bus tour of Saskatchewan as a surprise Christmas present for Mrs. Trudeau.

Mr. Trudeau will ask Pierre Cardin for a man's cologne that smells like perspiration.

And Mr. Trudeau will hire Toronto mayor William Dennison as his speech writer and Ontario Liberal leader Robert Nixon as his private tutor in charisma.

If all that won't change the PM's image, nothing will.

November 17, 1971

Getting the best possible deal for Canada

CANADA will have a lot at stake next week when Prime Minister Trudeau visits President Nixon in Washington.

To get the best possible deal for our country, how should Mr. Trudeau act?

Should the PM be humble and contrite, or bold and aggressive?

What kind of game plan do we need?

To get the answer, I called a Washington contact.

After listening to the problem, my informant said, "When Mr. Trudeau meets Mr. Nixon, the first thing he should do is kick him in the shins and then give a karate chop to the neck."

"Is that the way to win Mr. Nixon's friendship?" I gasped.

"Of course not," was the reply. "I didn't realize you wanted Mr. Nixon's friendship. I thought you wanted a better deal for Canada."

"We do," I responded.

"Then what you want is Mr. Nixon's wrath. Haven't you noticed what happens to his friends—Nationalist China, South Viet Nam, Britain, Italy and so on?

"They're either broke, bombed or bewildered."

"But if Mr. Trudeau mugs Mr. Nixon, won't the president retaliate by raising the surcharge and cutting off Canada completely?" I wanted to know.

"Exactly. And that solves your chief problem—unemployment," my source revealed.

"Without American imports, you'll have to produce Canadian goods. That means Canadian factories, Canadian coal, Canadian pipelines, Canadian shipping.

"You'll have to have Canadian unions, Canadian television, Canadian magazines, even a Canadian defence industry.

"That adds up to a lot of jobs."

"But . . ."

"A good kick on Mr. Nixon's shins would also improve your ecology.

"With no American market, your forests would last longer, you

59

wouldn't pollute your atmosphere producing power for New York City, and you'd have enough clean water to last yourselves for a thousand years."

"But . . ."

"You could trade those mothballed CF5 fighter planes to Israel for oranges, cut down traffic congestion by driving small European cars and recall Bobby Orr from the Boston Bruins and make him play for a Canadian team.

"It's the obvious answer," my Washington informant concluded.

"But you're an American," I pointed out. "Why are you telling me this?"

"Because we're sick of hearing Canadians whine," he said.

December 3, 1971

The inside story of how the Tories will match that baby

THIS COULD be an election year in Canada and the Conservatives are worried sick.

In fact, they called an emergency meeting recently in Bob Stanfield's office.

"Gentlemen," the chairman began, "we've got a crisis on our hands. If the nation goes to the polls in 1972, the Tory party could be wiped out."

Of course pandemonium reigned—and in buckets.

After order was restored, the chairman continued: "We've got ideas, leadership, snappy sayings and a promise from Dalton Camp he won't help in the next campaign.

"But there's one thing we haven't got."

"What's that?" a voice from the floor challenged.

"A baby," the chairman answered. "Our survey indicates Prime Minister Trudeau's popularity has taken a sharp upswing since he became a father at Christmas.

"Not only do Canadian voters love babies—they haven't missed

60

the significance of the Trudeau baby's birth on Christmas Day.

"They're afraid now if they vote against Trudeau he'll turn them into pillars of salt.

"There's even a rumor in Ottawa that the PM won't use television during the campaign.

"According to this report, Mr. Trudeau plans to speak to the Canadian public, coast to coast, from a burning bush."

"How can we fight back?" came the plea from a sobbing party official.

"Obviously we've got to have a baby of our own," the chairman revealed.

"With this in mind, next weekend we've booked the bridal suite at the Bide-a-Wee Motel and Bowling Lanes in Niagara Falls for Mr. and Mrs. Stanfield.

"The fate of the Tory party is in their hands."

All eyes turned to Mr. Stanfield who, up to this very moment, hadn't said a word.

Slowly the Opposition leader got up, cleared his throat and spoke.

"I accept the assignment," he announced.

After the applause had died down, the chairman mentioned: "By the way, Mr. Stanfield, to get the kind of impact we're after, we want the baby Easter Sunday."

"Easter? That's impossible," the Tory leader gasped. "Easter's only a few weeks away and . . ."

"Charlie, get Dief on the phone," the chairman said to an aide. "Tell him we've got a proposition for him."

January 5, 1972

61

Chapter 5:
Election 1972

Date of our election? Don't ask Trudeau, ask his son Justin

TOP-LEVEL talks have been held in Ottawa recently to pick a date for the next federal election.

Government officials have agonized long into the night, but so far no decision has been reached.

"There are two schools of thought in the Liberal party," a leading Grit confided to me. "One wants an election while the Prime Minister's baby is still in the crib kicking at butterflies.

"The other group feels we shouldn't ask the nation for a mandate until Justin learns to crawl.

"The party is split down the middle on this one."

"What dates are you looking at?" I wanted to know.

"If the plastic butterfly lobby gets its way, Canadians will probably vote in June.

"However, if the pro-crawl supporters win out, look for a fall election," my informant said.

"How do you feel about the issue?" was my next question.

"There are a great many advantages to running a political campaign with a baby under 6 months of age," he stated.

"For one thing, they get gas and smile a lot. You hardly ever get a bad picture of a baby under 6 months."

"It's something to think about," I agreed.

"There is a special serenity about a tiny baby being held in his mother's arms," my informant pointed out. "Even prairie voters might be touched.

"On the other hand, a baby just learning to crawl is terrific television. It has movement, excitement, even laughs.

"If we're lucky, Justin might get a tooth or a kiss curl in the middle of the race. Can you imagine what that would do to grandmothers coast to coast?

"Who knows, if we put off the election until October, Justin might even say goo-goo or da-da on network TV!

"It would ruin the Tories."

"A baby learning to crawl does tug at the heartstrings," I commented.

"Exactly. So we can play it safe with a 6-month-old, or go for broke with a pre-toddler."

"What will the PM do?" I demanded.

"I don't know," he replied. "But I've warned Ottawa if we don't decide soon we may have to consider other factors—like the economy."

February 25, 1972

How Ottawa aims to out-cool China during Nixon visit

THE FIRST official trip for President Richard Nixon since his historic tour of China will be to Canada next month.

Naturally, the boys in Ottawa feel the pressure.

They realize they'll have to come up with something special to make the Americans forget the Peking visit.

"It's a tough act to follow," an informant in our nation's capital confessed, "but we think we can pull it off."

"What have you in mind?" I asked.

"Do you remember what impressed Americans most about the welcome Mr. Nixon got in Peking?

"Let me tell you—it was the silence.

"Everywhere the president went, he was virtually ignored. It was one of the biggest stories of the tour.

"So we're training thousands of school children not to wave flags and not to applaud when Mr. Nixon arrives in Ottawa.

"The New York Times and Walter Cronkite will love it."

"There was more to the president's China trip than the snub at the airport," I pointed out.

"That's right," my source agreed. "A great deal of coverage was given to what Mrs. Nixon called 'that horrible Chinese liquor'."

"Do you mean the stuff used in Premier Chou En-lai's friendship toasts?"

"Exactly. Apparently it's 120 proof and tastes awful," was his reply.

"Unfortunately we don't have Chinese liquor—but we do have Newfie screech.

"We're confident it will burn as much as anything the Nixons drank in Peking."

"Have you arranged any ping pong tournaments?" I wanted to know.

"No, we can't beat the Americans at ping pong the way the Chinese did.

"However, we can whip them at street hockey so we've scheduled several games for Mr. Nixon while he's here."

"Are you sure the Americans really want a cool reception, bad liquor and some lop-sided defeats?" I questioned.

"It worked in China," he said. "Why shouldn't it work here?

"Now, if we can only get John Diefenbaker to look inscrutable and insult the president, I think we've covered everything."

March 28, 1972

A Trudeau questionnaire for enterprising writers

THE FOLLOWING questionnaire is being sent to reporters across the country:

1. Did you dance with Mr. Trudeau in the past 12 months?

2. Have you appeared with the PM on an open line radio show, TV panel or round-table discussion and asked him about unemployment or the Quebec question?

3. Has the Prime Minister sponsored you in a swimathon, walkathon, etc. and have you amusingly written about it for your readers?

4. Have you had an exclusive interview with the PM in which he didn't reveal the date of the next federal election under a page one headline?

5. Have you referred to the difference in ages between Mr. and

Mrs. Trudeau more than 75 times?

6. Have you carried an editorial page cartoon depicting the PM as Napoleon, Louis the Fourteenth, Rasputin or Marie Antoinette?

7. Did you write a feature for the women's pages in praise of Mrs. Trudeau when it was revealed she was breast-feeding Justin?

8. Have you accompanied Mr. Trudeau on a ski junket, a diplomatic mission or a honeymoon?

9. Have you personally been close enough to hear the PM use a swear word?

10. Did you ever hold Mr. Trudeau's coat while he cut a ribbon, opened a building, kicked a football, or visited a hospital?

11. Have you written a 10-part series on the PM's charisma?

12. Have you ever tried to telephone Mr. Trudeau's barber, ex-girlfriends, caterer, judo instructor, former classmates, or his religious adviser to get information on what Mr. Trudeau is really like?

13. Have you written Mrs. Trudeau to ask for the PM's favorite recipe, color, music, etc.?

14. Have you had your picture taken with the PM on Parliament Hill, at an ethnic picnic, in his office, in your office, at a car-wash opening?

15. Have you taken a survey among your listeners, viewers or readers to see what they think about Mr. Trudeau's hair length?

16. Did you hold a name-the-baby contest when Mrs. Trudeau was expecting?

17. Have you done an in-depth story on the PM's astrological chart? His handwriting?

18. Have you obtained an article of the PM's clothing to be raffled off for a good cause by a local charity?

19. Have you made more than 35 speeches this year on What Effect Marriage Has Had On Mr. Trudeau's Sex Appeal For The Masses?

20. Did you ever close your eyes when the PM kissed you on the cheek? Or vice versa?

The communications industry isn't optimistic but it hopes to find a journalist who can answer no to all 20 questions.

They want to name him or her reporter-of-the-year.

May 17, 1972

Margaret Trudeau looks dowdy—but there's a sneaky reason

THE OTHER DAY Canadian newspapers carried a photograph of Prime Minister Trudeau and his wife, Margaret, vacationing near Banff.

In the picture, the PM was as swashbuckling as ever—pirate shirt, rumpled jeans, hat pulled at a rakish angle over one ear.

But Mrs. Trudeau?

Frankly, she looked matronly. Baggy men's trousers. Poor posture. Kerchief around her hair.

She looked old enough, well, old enough to be the PM's wife.

When they were married nearly two years ago, Mrs. Trudeau was gorgeous, smashing and dazzling.

And now she looks like any other Canadian woman with a small child.

Is that what living with Mr. Trudeau has done to her?

"Not at all," a Liberal strategist informed me. "Under those ill-fitting clothes and slouch, there's still a beautiful woman.

"But we're trying to keep it secret until after the election."

"Why's that?" I asked.

"Our surveys indicate many Canadian women were jealous of Mrs. Trudeau when she married the PM.

"There she was—young, slender, terrific figure, great smile.

"With all that going against her, we realized immediately she could never be popular with other women.

"So, rather than risk alienating 50 per cent of the electorate, we asked Mrs. Trudeau if she'd mind taking a crash course in being plain."

"What did that consist of?" was my next question.

"We taught her to stand round-shouldered, to throw on a lifejacket whenever a photographer came around and to borrow some of Jean Marchand's old suits for public appearances.

"The result, as you pointed out, is the picture splashed across the front page of several Canadian dailies.

"For the first time since her marriage, Margaret Trudeau has won the affection of Canadian housewives.

"That unflattering profile shot was probably worth at least 200,000 votes to the Liberals."

"But how will male voters react?" I inquired.

"Favorably," the strategist responded. "Now that they think Mr. Trudeau sees the same thing across the breakfast table every morning as they do, he'll get a big sympathy vote."

August 10, 1972

They want to know why charm, kisses missing on hustings

MANY LIBERALS are baffled by Prime Minister Trudeau's "low key" approach to the Oct. 30 election.

They want to know why he hasn't turned on the charm and kisses that featured his 1968 campaign.

To get the answer, I called my favorite Ottawa contact.

"What Liberals forget," he chided, "is that the Prime Minister is four years older than he was during the last federal election."

"Are you suggesting that his pucker has gone downhill in the past four years?" I asked.

"Hasn't yours?" he replied. "To use the vernacular of the sports world, the PM is definitely a lip slower this year.

"When he was 48 and in his prime, Mr. Trudeau could go to a rally and easily kiss 250 women during an appearance, 300 if they were good looking.

"He was one of those candidates who comes along once in a lifetime—a natural kisser.

"I once saw him deliver 12 pecks, four nibbles, eight smacks and a sigh without taking a second breath.

"Not only that, the PM was a switch-kisser; he could tilt his head to either the left or the right—it didn't matter to him. He seemed to know instinctively where the noses went.

"Yes, Mr. Trudeau was the consummate pro when it came to bussing.

"But that, as I say, was in 1968 when his powers of osculation were at their peak."

"So the past four years have taken their toll on our leader's mouth!"

"Exactly. That, and marriage."

"Are you suggesting the Prime Minister would be more high-powered on the hustings if it wasn't for his marriage?"

"Of course. It's difficult to walk the floor all night with Justin and then rush off first thing in the morning to face a line-up of 5,000 women, all standing with their chins up and their eyes closed.

"You need your sleep if you want to be charismatic and sexy.

"On top of that, there's one other problem."

"What's that?"

"If Pierre comes home at night with 7,856 different shades of lipstick on his shirt collar, Margaret will kill him."

October 11, 1972

Experts called in to give lessons in humility

CANADIAN voters have indicated they don't care who is prime minister, provided he's humble.

As a result, an amazing transformation is taking place in Ottawa these days.

Experts from across the land have been called in to give Pierre Trudeau humility lessons.

"We realize now Canadians don't want an exciting, confident, debonair leader," a Liberal contact informed me.

"What they want is someone who is chastened, contrite and modest.

"Unfortunately, Mr. Trudeau doesn't have as much to be modest about as Mr. Stanfield or Mr. Lewis.

"Therefore, we have to work much harder than the Tories and the NDP to project this image of mediocrity and lack of confidence."

"How are you going about it?" I asked.

"In a dozen ways," he responded. "For one thing, we've instructed the PM to tone down his mind.

"He'll never get anywhere if he keeps insisting on topping reporters at press conferences, especially in two languages."

"That's a good point," I agreed. "Journalists don't like to think anyone's better qualified to run the country than they are. It makes them uneasy."

"Exactly. So we're giving Mr. Trudeau a crash course in platitudes. With the right sort of encouragement, we're sure he can be as boring as any run-of-the-mill politician.

"Of course we're not overlooking his strong leadership either," my informant added.

"By making decisions—right or wrong—and running the cabinet as if he were in charge, Mr. Trudeau offended a lot of people."

"He was a little bossy," I agreed.

"We can see that now. The key to survival in Canadian politics is evasiveness. It's the wishy-washy who inherit the land.

"What we're trying to get across to Mr. Trudeau is this: Whenever he feels like being witty, clever, sophisticated or decisive, he should lie down until the feeling goes away."

"How is Mr. Trudeau fitting in to his new image?" I asked.

"Not very well yet. He still quotes Oriental philosophers if you don't watch him and he comes up with an insight now and then.

"But we have to be patient.

"As I told him just the other day, Mr. Stanfield and Mr. Lewis didn't become nonentities overnight either."

November 8, 1972

Nixon to Trudeau:
"Please speak...
...into pen stand"

WE'VE LEARNED that President Nixon has bugged even his own office for the past four-and-a-half years.

According to Watergate testimony, the president wanted a record of his discussions in the White House "for historical reasons."

That's a noble motive.

However, you can't help wondering how the presence of a recorder affected conversation in the Oval room.

It's a fact of life that a person doesn't talk the same when he knows his words are being taken down on tape—and for posterity.

So how did President Nixon, for example, greet our own Prime Minister Trudeau, knowing full well that future generations were listening in to every syllable?

The meeting probably went like this.

"Good morning—comma—Prime Minister Trudeau—capital P, M and T period and new paragraph.

"It's good to see you here in the White House—capital W and H—on this beautiful morning in the year of 1971—check for the exact date—it's either Dec. 5 or 6."

"It's good to see you, too, Mr. President, and..."

"Just a moment, Mr. Prime Minister, I'm not finished.

"Eliminate above and pick up at Dec. 5 or 6.

"Paragraph.

"As president of this great republic—comma—it gives me special pleasure to welcome you as the representative of that great nation to our north—dash—Canada—C-A-N-A-D-A.

"New paragraph.

"For 200 years our countries have lived in peace along an undefended border 3,000 miles long—semi-colon—and that is a record we can be proud of—no, change that to a record of which we can be proud.

"Paragraph.

71

"So—comma—I say to you—comma—welcome—exclamation mark. End of statement."

"Are you feeling all right, Mr. President?"

"Of course."

"Then I may continue?"

"By all means, Mr. Prime Minister. But just one small suggestion. When you speak, speak directly into my pen stand.

"And please—don't slur your words.

"Okay—roll tape!"

July 19, 1973

Here's play-by-play of Pierre Trudeau discovering the West

A GREAT moment in Canadian history took place a few days ago in Vancouver.

Not all of us could be present in person but, fortunately, Foster Hewitt was there for the play-by-play.

We switch you now to Foster...

"Hello history fans from coast to coast and Newfoundland. This is Foster Hewitt speaking to you from the gondola high above Vancouver harbor.

"The Ottawa team headed by Pierre Trudeau hasn't appeared on the water as yet but they're expected momentarily.

"With me to describe the action is my color commentator, one of the great voices of radio and TV, my son, Bill.

"This is a great moment, Bill. You can almost feel the tension building here."

"That's right, dad."

"Thanks for that observation, Bill. The Ottawa team will be at the south end to our left when they—here they come now.

"As far as I can make out, there are three canoes and it appears that Mr. Trudeau is kneeling in the bow of the first one.

"Yes, he's definitely kneeling. And he's got his right hand up shading his eyes.

72

"Bill, would you describe the Ottawa uniform as buckskin shirts and trousers, moccasins and coonskin hats?"

"Yes, I would, dad."

"That's an interesting comment, Bill. The Ottawa club is paddling about 100 yards from shore, coming directly toward us. They're still coming.

"The crowd has just let up a cheer and Mr. Trudeau is waving something in his hand.

"From here it looks like trinkets and beads. The canoes are getting closer to shore—they've landed on the beach.

"Ladies and gentlemen, Mr. Trudeau has just discovered western Canada!

"It's a wonderful moment, Bill, and the history fans here are littering the harbor with programs, hats and galoshes."

"They sure are, dad.'

"Excuse me, Bill, but we're going to try to get Mr. Trudeau to our microphone to say a few words.

"Pardon me, Mr. Trudeau, but how does it feel to have just discovered western Canada?"

"Western Canada! Isn't this China?"

"And now back to you Bill for our three-star selection..."

July 20, 1973

Trudeau and Mao—two humble men meet

PRIME MINISTER Pierre Trudeau may be granted the highest honor the Chinese can pay a visiting dignitary—a private meeting with Chairman Mao.

Frankly, I'm worried.

According to reports from Peking, Chairman Mao is a humble man just brimming with that most prized of all Oriental virtues—humility.

Well, that describes our PM, too.

Worried that some people might think him arrogant, Trudeau has been on a modesty kick ever since last autumn's election.

Well, what do two humble men talk about when they get together? It could go like this . . .

"Good morning, Chairman Mao. I can't tell you how much I've looked forward to this meeting."

"Ah, Mr. Trudeau, and I have looked forward to this meeting even more than you."

"Please permit me to disagree, Chairman Mao. I am a simple, unworthy man from far-off Canada. I'm sure I've looked forward to this meeting more than you have."

"China is a tiny apple, Canada a vast orchard, Mr. Trudeau. It is you who have done me a great honor. And may I say how well you look?"

"Not half as well as you, Chairman Mao. You are the picture of health and I am insignificant in comparison."

"No, I am the insignificant one, Mr. Trudeau. I am old and weak and worn out. I am sure you could beat any world leader in a foot race."

"Perhaps I could outrun Mr. Nixon or Mrs. Ghandi—but I could never match you, Chairman Mao. I saw the photographs of you swimming and my inferiority makes me blush."

"The bird who flies fastest does not always soar highest in sky, Mr. Trudeau, and greatness is not always obvious to the human eye, especially in those suffering from astigmatism."

"May I write that down, Chairman Mao? I would like to live the rest of my life by that creed. You're so humble it makes me want to cry."

"You, too, are humble, Mr. Trudeau."

"You are at least 100 times more humble than this lowly personage, Chairman Mao."

"You are too generous, exalted guest. But enough. We must join the others. After you, Mr. Trudeau."

"No, venerable sage, after you."

"I insist, distinguished visitor, after you."

"Please, glowing presence. Teacher before pupil, saint before sinner, enlightened man before . . ."

"All right, Mr. Trudeau. I'll go first. But do me a favor."

"Anything, light of the Orient."

"Will you knock it off if I promise to give you a panda bear?"

October 12, 1973

74

Chapter 6: Election 1974

Time for Tory self-controls

W ITH THE federal election only days away, a serious rift has developed in the nation.

Everyone agrees inflation is no laughing matter but there is a serious difference of opinion on how it can be cured.

Conservative leader Robert Stanfield says Canada is doomed unless we adopt price-and-wage controls.

Prime Minister Trudeau, on the other hand, claims such a freeze won't work.

That leaves the rest of us in the middle. What do we do?

The Prime Minister is no fool. However, Mr. Stanfield has been to college, too, and knows John Bassett personally.

And yet we have to decide which to follow, knowing full well a misplaced X could wipe out this generation, not to mention those to follow.

It's an awesome responsibility, especially for people like myself who never did quite master the mysteries of long division, let alone pierce the complexities of international high finance.

Personally, with the country in such dire straits, I feel it's time for Mr. Stanfield and his followers to rise above the pettiness of politics.

This is a time for boldness and attack.

To show his sincerity (if there's any doubt) Mr. Stanfield should go on record now as stating he and every other Tory in the country will accept self-imposed price-and-wage controls, regardless of the outcome of the July 8 election.

Let the Grits, socialists and others do it their way.

The Tories (so Mr. Stanfield should state) will not raise prices in their shops, accept wage increases, nor will they cash dividend checks above present levels.

Of course it would be better (if Mr. Stanfield's theory is correct) if every last one of us promised the same.

However, if there are seven or eight million Conservatives in Canada, as some polls indicate, that should at least help cool down the spiralling cost of living.

You can imagine how embarrassing it would be to Mr. Trudeau if his government (and its policies) are returned to office and inflation slows to a walk in areas where the Conservatives are concentrated.

There could be no arguing that and Mr. Trudeau, after four or five years of having the lesson drummed home, would undoubtedly retire from politics, blushing profusely, ready to admit he was wrong to Mr. Stanfield in person.

It's a wonderful opportunity for the Conservatives to put our money where their mouth is and I hope they don't blow it.

I also hope our plumber is a Tory.

July 2, 1974

Nobody was at home when he phoned P.E.I.

AN ESTIMATED $50 million has been spent on the current election campaign; about 57,876 speeches have been made; and the newspapers have carried approximately 5,678 tons of political tidbits, anecdotes and cartoons.

Now only one question remains: Will any Canadians turn up July 8 at the polls to vote?

"We're hoping to have a turnout of between 75 and 80," an election official in Ottawa revealed to me in an exclusive interview.

"Per cent?" I asked.

"No, people," was his reply.

"How did you get that figure?"

"We made a survey and, at last count, 80 Canadians have given us their word they'll show up at the polls on Monday.

"Of course weather could be a factor so I like to say 75, just to be on the safe side."

"Where is interest highest?"

"Ontario. In our telephone poll we got 37 'definitely interested' responses and 6 'possibly may vote if we don't go to the cottage' replies.

"On the other hand, we phoned Prince Edward Island and

nobody was home."

"It would be wrong then to suggest the country was caught up in the election fever?"

"That's right. Not only are we unable to detect signs of fever, we're not even sure the country is breathing. There's a distinct possibility the electorate passed away several weeks ago and forgot to tell the candidates."

"Why is the nation a-buzz with apathy?"

"For one thing, Canadians have a bigger problem on their hands at this time of year: How do you start a barbecue short of buying a flame-thrower from war surplus and marinating your wienie overnight in hi-test gasoline?"

"Each of our national leaders makes a good speech," I pointed out.

"That's true. Unfortunately, they keep repeating it over and over. Mr. Stanfield is the record-holder. He's made his same speech 378 times—which is 11 times more often than Mr. Trudeau has repeated his speech."

"What about Mr. Lewis?"

"At last count, Mr. Lewis had made his speech 789 times. However, it's not a record since he's used his text in both the 1972 and 1974 elections and the record book clearly states a speech must be delivered during the same campaign to qualify."

"Is there any other reason for mass indifference?"

"In discussing the situation, we have learned that Canadians consider elections like streetcars. If you miss one, there's another along in a few minutes."

"Well, in spite of all the apathy, you can put me down as definitely going to vote on Monday," I said. "What time do the polls open?"

"What time can you be there?" he asked.

July 4, 1974

The next time I have a scoop I'll write it

DURING the 1972 federal campaign, Senator Keith Davey called up to ask whether I'd like to hear Marc Lalonde speak at a luncheon at the Royal York Hotel. I agreed—on the premise that a person should try everything once, even a Liberal meeting.

After the lunch, Keith offered to drive me back to the office, but when we got to his car in the parking lot, he started to talk.

"I don't like the way Mr. Trudeau is running in this campaign," he said.

"He should be telling the Canadian people he wants the job, that being Prime Minister is very important to him. That's not how he's coming across. He seems to be saying, 'Here I am, if you want me.'"

I made a half-hearted defence of the Trudeau "cool," but Keith plunged on.

"I don't like the way it's going," he said. "Trudeau isn't concentrating enough in the Toronto area either.

"Do you know something? He doesn't feel comfortable here the way he does in Montreal. He feels like a stranger. But he should be zeroing in on Toronto because it could be the key to victory."

For almost half an hour we talked about the '72 campaign—at least Keith Davey did. He was very pessimistic.

At first I put it down to the fact that this was the first federal campaign he hadn't managed since the pre-Pearson days.

He obviously missed the smoke-filled rooms, the party intrigues, the long hours away from home, the tension and the savage in-fighting, just the way some people long to go over Niagara Falls in a barrel.

"I'm going to write Trudeau and tell him exactly what I think," he confided. "We're making too many mistakes."

Some months later, after the no-decision election of 1972, I heard that Davey would mastermind the next Liberal campaign.

And of course, that's what he did.

Everything he talked about that afternoon in the hotel parking lot became part of the Liberal strategy in the 1974 election—the tougher, more dedicated Trudeau; the focus on Toronto; and even the return to influence of the "pros" within the Liberal party. (Yes, Davey mentioned that, too.)

It all happened.

And I had the scoop back in 1972—at least 18 months ahead of everyone else.

Of course I didn't write a single word about it.

Sometimes I don't think I'll ever make the grade in this business.

July 10, 1974

Stanfield and Lewis: We love them now

WITHOUT QUESTION, the most beloved politicians in the country today are David Lewis and Bob Stanfield. They can do no wrong.

The media adore them, the public thinks they're super, and everyone agrees it would be a severe blow if either decides to quit public life.

With so much affection on their side, the question naturally arises: Why didn't Mr. Stanfield and Mr. Lewis get more votes in last Monday's election?

To get an answer to this interesting puzzle, I talked to the political pundit at our office.

"The first thing you have to understand is that their popularity is based on unpopularity," he began.

I must have looked puzzled, because he went on.

"Look, the only reason the Canadian public accepts them today is because the public rejected them this week.

"Canadians love losers. As soon as Mr. Lewis and Mr. Stanfield were wiped out at the polls, their popularity shot up 500 per cent.

"At this moment, about 75 per cent of all Canadians have a warm, tender feeling in their hearts for Mr. Stanfield and Mr.

Lewis. It could have been 85 or 90 per cent if they hadn't done so well in the prairie provinces."

"What kind of popularity did they have before the election?"

"Their popularity was on the upswing until the first public opinion polls came out indicating they were gathering support and might even form the next government.

"Naturally, as soon as the public saw it might be backing a winner, they immediately rejected Mr. Stanfield and Mr. Lewis and went back to Mr. Trudeau who looked as if he might be the loser.

"That was probably the deciding factor in the election. Thousands of Canadians voted for Mr. Trudeau just because they thought Mr. Stanfield or Mr. Lewis would be Prime Minister and they felt sorry for Mr. Trudeau."

"How do they feel now?"

"Disappointed, of course. They assumed they were siding with the underdog and wound up backing a majority government instead.

"That's why they're so pro-Stanfield and pro-Lewis today."

"Does that mean Mr. Trudeau's popularity is at a low ebb again?"

"I'm afraid so," the pundit replied.

"That mandate from the people just about kills whatever chances he had for public acceptance."

"Oh, well, there's always a next time in politics," I said.

July 15, 1974

Nixon wasn't talking about Trudeau at all!

ALMOST HALF of all Canadians were upset to learn ex-president Nixon referred to our Prime Minister as "asshole Trudeau" during a 1973 White House meeting with his advisers. Even a few Tories think it's hitting below the belt.

However, my Washington sources insist Mr. Nixon never used

that vulgar phrase in reference to Mr. Trudeau.

"As usual, the press has it wrong," my informant stated.

"How can you say that?" I asked over the telephone. "It's right there on the Watergate tapes. And, if that's not enough, there are witnesses—Bob Haldeman, John Ehrlichman and John Mitchell.

"They all heard Mr. Nixon say, 'asshole Trudeau.'"

"They may have thought they heard it but they didn't," he insisted.

"I don't believe you," I said. "It was even quoted in The Toronto Star."

"Well, if you don't want to hear the real story . . . "

"No, go on. What's your explanation?"

"Very simple. It's very true Mr. Nixon was in his office March 22, 1973, with the people you mentioned. They were discussing the nation's business when the president mentioned he was entertaining the Japanese ambassador at a private dinner that evening.

"As you know, Mr. Nixon was very keen on developing trade relations with Tokyo so, to make certain the Japanese ambassador felt at home, the president hired a special caterer just for the evening—a Mr. Ah So whose specialty is sukiyaki.

"Unfortunately, the regular White House chef felt insulted by the intrusion and, apparently, tried to give the caterer a hard time.

"Mr. Nixon was worried because the White House chef had insulted the caterer, deliberately dropped a carving knife on his foot, put salt in the sugar bowl, and tried to lock the poor man in the freezer.

"The president didn't know how much more the Japanese caterer would take before striking back.

"At that very moment there was the sound of a terrific fight from downstairs and the telephone rang.

"Mr. Nixon answered and turned white. Somebody—Haldeman, I think—asked what happened.

"The president stared at his advisers and gasped, 'Ah So threw dough!'"

"And that's been garbled to 'asshole Trudeau'?" I asked.

"Exactly," my informant said. "And anyone who says otherwise is a twit."

October 25, 1974

Getting the scoop at 24 Sussex Drive

MARGARET TRUDEAU has decided to become a reporter-photographer. Yes, at long last, Canada is going to have an Anthony Armstrong-Jones of its own.

Chatelaine magazine is going to run Mrs. Trudeau's first photo-story in its February or March issue. Naturally, many of us are eagerly awaiting it because Margaret has advantages the rest of the press doesn't possess.

In fact, now that Margaret has become a journalist, this is how the scene may develop at 24 Sussex Drive, after Pierre gets home from a hard day at the office.

"Hello, dear. You look terribly tired. Did something go wrong with the country today?"

"Something? Everything. How about fixing me a drink—a martini, very dry."

"Of course, Pierre—after you tell me what went on between Canada and the Arab bloc today."

"Can't I have the drink first?"

"No scoopee, no drinkee, Pierre."

"Margaret, can't you forget your new job for just one evening and let me relax?"

"Pierre, I need a big story to put me in solid with the editors at Chatelaine. If I come up with an exclusive, they'll give me my own byline and maybe even a chance to write a series of articles on crumbly desserts or what it's like to watch daytime TV at 24 Sussex Drive.

"Besides, it's worth $300 to me."

"Very well, Margaret. We seem to be making progress with the Arabs on an oil deal but nothing's signed. Now can I have my drink?"

"Certainly—just as soon as I write that down. Would you mind holding that pose, by the way? I'd like to catch you at f4 with a shutter speed of one-60th."

"Margaret, I'm still waiting for my drink."

"I'll make it a double if you tell me what you said to Eugene

Whelan today at the cabinet meeting. And, if it's really sensational, I'll throw in your favorite dinner—pot roast."

"Margaret, last night you wouldn't give me my dessert until I told you what I really thought of former president Nixon.

"The day before that you wouldn't iron my shirts unless I let you look around RCMP headquarters in Ottawa and take photographs of the counter-intelligence section.

"When will it end? How long will you continue to blackmail me like this?"

"If you tell me what John Turner is really like, I'll make out the Christmas cards this year, Pierre, AND vacuum the front room rug."

"Forget about the drink. I'm going to bed."

"Of course, Pierre, but first . . ."

November 18, 1974

Trudeay (sob) wastes our best rude words

PRIME MINISTER Trudeau's latest outburst in Parliament may have cost him the support of one of this country's most powerful minority groups—the Save Our Bombast (SOB) society.

While their numbers aren't large, there are SOBs in every province, often in high places.

And they have one aim—to preserve the integrity of swear words in everyday conversation.

According to an SOB spokesman, Trudeau has done more to debase profanity than any other Canadian of our time.

"Every time the PM gets annoyed at somebody, he calls him a swear word," my contact complained. "Naturally, every SOB resents this sort of overkill.

"We feel profanity should be used in moderation. That way it maintains its impact."

"But the PM was mad," I pointed out.

"You can't go around cursing everyone who annoys you, or

looks sideways across the House of Commons floor," was his answer.

"For heaven's sake, the way Mr. Trudeau throws around profanity, pretty soon there won't be a swear word that hasn't been splashed across the front page or shouted from car radios into the ears of every Brownie and old lady coast to coast.

"It may be fine in the short range—funny, good reading in the paper and so on. But what about the long term effects?

"When we really need a strong word to express our disgust or dismay, will there be one left in the gutter—or will Mr. Trudeau have used them all up?"

"You've got a point," I conceded, "but what would you suggest Mr. Trudeau use to insult his opponents in the meantime?"

"There's no reason why he couldn't have called Harvie Andre a twit, boob or lout," he answered.

"If he was really hot under the collar, the PM could have muttered that the Tory backbencher was gross AND a nincompoop.

"That certainly is damaging enough—and yet it falls short of profanity. It does not erode the clout of our really rude words."

"Have you thought of telling Mr. Trudeau to his face?" I inquired.

"Yes, but we're afraid he'd tell us to—ahem—fuddle duddle, and that would only set back our cause.

"All we can do," he added, "is sit back and hope Mr. Trudeau one day stops talking like an American president."

November 27, 1974

Maryon, come home to 24 Sussex Drive

MANY CANADIANS have had difficulty accepting a prime minister's wife who wears T-shirts on state visits, sings at diplomatic receptions and goes on open-line radio programs to discuss her personal feelings.

Those same people are now having just as much trouble living with an Opposition leader's wife who insists on using her maiden name, attends college and is only 23 years of age.

"Apparently we face the choice of either Margaret Trudeau or Ms Maureen McTeer as our first lady," one bewildered and disgruntled citizen of advanced (37) years stated to me.

"Frankly, we feel the job should go to somebody with more experience, somebody with a more conventional life style, in short, somebody who more reflects the taste of the average Canadian."

"What do you have in mind?" I asked.

"Some of us have got together and started a draft-Maryon-Pearson-or-Olive-Diefenbaker movement.

"We don't intend to rest until Maryon or Olive is back where she belongs, at 24 Sussex Drive, pouring tea, avoiding the spotlight, and wearing a nice double-knit suit with a brooch at the shoulder."

"You've got to give the next generation a chance," I suggested.

"We don't mind having a young Prime Minister or leader of the Opposition," the leader of the draft-Maryon-or-Olive movement argued, "but we don't want the real power in the country to be handed over to a slip of a girl in blue jeans.

"Canada is too big to be run by somebody who has homework to do after 4.

"What we need at the helm is an authentic mother-figure, not somebody who wants to cut out early from the embassy dinner so she can get home in time to watch Fonzi on television."

"Margaret Trudeau has called herself an educated chick, and I'm sure Ms McTeer is just as bright and sophisticated," I protested.

"That's probably why we need a Maryon Pearson or Olive Diefenbaker back in the drawing rooms of power. One look and you know you don't have to worry about them bouncing a ball off the Parliament buildings' walls while waiting for their husbands to finish work."

"You're going to be accused of being prejudiced against youth," was my next comment.

"Look, when they can dismiss Claude Wagner at 50 as over-the-hill and old, those of us who don't happen to use Clearasil or go to camp in the summer are entitled to take a few cracks at people in the 20-year-old age bracket," my contact stated.

"You've got a point," I conceded. "Do you think Mrs. Pearson or Mrs. Diefenbaker will accept a draft?"

"Nobody with a little gray in her hair and her second teeth could refuse the challenge," rang out the reply. "What Canada needs on the front porch at 24 Sussex Drive is a rocker, not a swinger.

"Remember when Olive Diefenbaker used to knit in the dark because Dief wanted to go to bed early and the light bothered him?

"Remember when Maryon Pearson used to sit through an entire banquet and never open her mouth?"

"Those were the days!"

February 26, 1975

"Tell it like it isn't" people beg Trudeau

BANKERS, union leaders, chamber of commerce spokesmen and representatives of big business have attacked Prime Minister Trudeau for stating the free market system in Canada isn't working.

Obviously, if Trudeau wants to get these powerful interests behind him, he should make a speech something like this:

"Good evening, and thank you for inviting me to your meeting so I can have the opportunity of making a few comments to you this evening about the state of the nation.

"Happily, I can report that things in Canada have never been better. The free market system as we know it is functioning perfectly and, from B.C. to Newfoundland, I'm delighted to say we shouldn't change a single thing.

"Canada, my friends, is doing everything right."

(Applause, applause)

"First of all, inflation has been licked throughout the land and no longer constitutes a threat to our fiscal well-being.

"But, if you've been shopping at the supermarket or pricing a new car or hiring someone to fix your toilet, I don't have to tell you that.

"You know high prices are no concern to Canadians, as they are in Britain, Japan and some of those South American countries.

"Next, let me address myself to labor problems.

"It is with great satisfaction I can stand here this evening and tell you we don't have any.

"Our present free market system has eliminated labor unrest, done away with costly strikes, provided full employment and given every Canadian a fair share of the nation's treasure.

"It may sound immodest but other countries envy Canada's work record and labor harmony, and continually bombard my office for our secret."

(Applause, applause).

"And our record in energy is just as fantastic. Unlike the United States or the Netherlands, Canada has no need to change its present attitude to energy.

"Just as with our other natural resources, we are using our energy supply to perfection, and for the life of me I can't think of a single way we can improve over the system we have now.

"That goes for the way we use our farm land, our fresh water and the air we breathe, too.

"Canadians have nothing to learn from anyone and, if we leave things just the way they are, we haven't a single thing to worry about."

(Applause, applause).

"In conclusion, let me congratulate all of our vested interests from the lowliest banker to the highest union leader for helping make Canada what it is today, a land without problems, a land where happiness abounds, a land where any sort of change is unthinkable because the past has worked so well.

"Let us all thank God the crises of the rest of the world don't concern us, and Canada's future is guaranteed.

"And now, since everything is perfect, I'd like to play a selection on my violin. . ."

Apparently that's the kind of speech bankers, the chamber of commerce, union leaders and big business want Trudeau to deliver.

1974 and 1975—forever!

January 21, 1976

Trudeau's private life leaves us all guessing

EVERY SO OFTEN Prime Minister Trudeau disappears for 24 hours. All his office will say is that he's enjoying a "private" day, so naturally Canadians are dying with curiosity.

Where does the PM go? What does he do? Does he say "Shazam!" and vanish in a puff of smoke, or is it a trick done with mirrors?

Golly, no one knows.

After some thought, I've come up with several possibilities.

1. Prime Minister Trudeau is up in the mountains, examining the entrails of a reporter to see what the future holds for his administration.

2. Prime Minister Trudeau is busy in the basement at 24 Sussex Dr., chiselling out his next speech on stone tablets.

3. Prime Minister Trudeau is helping Margaret with the ironing.

4. Prime Minister Trudeau is in Defence Minister Richardson's garage, building the kites that will form Canada's Atlantic anti-submarine patrol now that the Lockheed deal has fallen through.

5. Prime Minister Trudeau is visiting relatives on the planet Krypton.

6. Prime Minister Trudeau is at his summer cottage attempting to start a fire by rubbing two cabinet ministers together.

7. Prime Minister Trudeau is trying to break Justin, Sacha and Michel of the habit of drinking water after he's walked on it.

8. Prime Minister Trudeau is knitting a muffler for Elmer McKay's mouth.

9. Prime Minister Trudeau is giving Jean Marchand driving lessons.

10. Prime Minister Trudeau is busy writing Senator Keith Davey's memoirs.

11. Prime Minister Trudeau is vacuuming the pool at 24 Sussex Dr.

12. Prime Minister Trudeau is on the phone telling Premier Bourassa that he's sorry but he doesn't have an extra $900,000,000 to spare 'til payday.

13. Prime Minister Trudeau is holding secret meetings with the RCMP, the results of which will not be revealed to the public until the early editions of tomorrow's newspapers.

14. Prime Minister Trudeau is home suffering an attack of Alberta gas.

15. Prime Minister Trudeau is down at the labor temple drawing moustaches on posters of Joe Morris.

16. Prime Minister Trudeau is taking Margaret out to lunch, trying to persuade her to take him along on her next tour of South America, Cuba, Europe, etc.

17. Prime Minister Trudeau is attempting to talk the bailiff out of seizing Quebec.

18. Prime Minister Trudeau is at Berlitz learning how to say "shove it" in 17 different languages.

19. Prime Minister Trudeau is at Mirabel airport still waiting to present a bouquet of flowers and a scroll to the 100th person to use the $500 million facility that opened six months ago.

20. Prime Minister Trudeau is in his study trying to learn the name of the Leader of the Opposition.

And that's what our PM may do on his "private" day.

May 25, 1976

Trudeau's troubles can't help Joe Clark

PRIME MINISTER Trudeau's popularity is at an all-time low. In fact, only 29 per cent of Canadians now approve of the way he's running the country.

Over 70 per cent want him out.

"It now appears the Conservatives are practically a cinch to form the next government," a contact in our nation's capital explained, "providing the Tories learn from Trudeau's mistakes."

Of course I begged for an explanation.

"When asked why they don't like the Prime Minister, the anti-Trudeau faction gave five chief reasons.

"They don't like him because he opposed capital punishment, brought in price-and-wage controls, supported French as this country's other language, and because he refused to let Taiwan compete in the Olympics under the name and flag of China," he explained.

"That's only four reasons for not liking Trudeau," I pointed out.

"Oh, yes and his critics claim he didn't stand straight enough at the Montreal games during the playing of the national anthem.

"According to the polls, those are the chief complaints expressed by the 71 per cent of Canadians who don't like him any more and think he's the pits."

"Perhaps that's true," I conceded, "but what's that got to do with the Conservatives? Surely it's a Liberal problem."

"Obviously, if Joe Clark wants to lead his party to power, he'll have to run on a platform promising hanging, unrestricted inflation, English-only, immediate recognition of Taiwan as the official government of mainland China and straight shoulders during the playing of O Canada."

"That doesn't sound like a very attractive ticket to run on," I commented. "Personally, I don't think Joe Clark would make promises like that."

"What's the alternative?" my source inquired. "At this very moment, if you believe the polls, nearly 10 million Canadian voters think Trudeau is doing a crummy job and give those reasons why.

"Apparently any politician who refuses to string up criminals or puts French on boxes of breakfast cereal is just asking for trouble."

"That certainly does put a lot of pressure on the Conservatives and the NDP," I gasped.

"Can you imagine running on a ticket that promises Vote Tory and Let Big Business And Big Labor Charge What They Want?" he asked. "Or, Go NDP and Stamp Out The Language Rights of 6 million Canadians Who Were Here First?"

"I'm not even sure I'd want to stand up on a platform and give my word that, if elected, my first act would be to infuriate 800 million Chinese," I confessed.

"The Canadian political scene does look bleak right now," my informant grumbled, "except for one thing."

"And what's that?" I asked, looking for even a crumb.

"The Carter-Ford debates," he replied. "They could be the salvation of our politicians.

"After watching Jimmy Carter and President Ford on television, our politicians don't look so bad after all.

"In fact, it wouldn't surprise me if some Canadians forgive Trudeau for speaking several languages fluently, even if one of them is French."

September 28, 1976

Was Trudeau right in saying "Hello"?

THE OTHER DAY Prime Minister Trudeau said "Hello" while welcoming Prime Minister Manley of Jamaica to Ottawa.

Undoubtedly the quote, like all Trudeau quotes, will become the center of another bitter national controversy.

Here is just a sample of the letters-to-the-editor that will appear soon across the nation in your favorite dailies.

To the editor:

Trudeau's recent "Hello" statement is just one more example of the man's astonishing arrogance. Does he say "Good day" as any normal human being would, or "Pleased to meet you"? No. He dismisses a major visitor to this country with a flip "Hello."

Surely Canadians need no more proof that this man must go before his aloofness and bad manners do irreparable damage to this country.

Concerned Citizen

To the editor:

How come Trudeau found time to attend the reception? Was the swimming pool at 24 Sussex Dr. being vacuumed?

Former Liberal Supporter

To the editor:

Trudeau's greeting to the foreign visitor to this country was widely quoted as being "Hello," but I have a second cousin who knows the hat check person in an important Ottawa hotel and he claims Trudeau's actual greeting was "'allo."

How much longer do we have to stand by and have the French language stuffed down our throats? It's bad enough to read it on the flakes at the breakfast table, but does this man have to resort to a foreign tongue every chance he gets?

Loyal Canadian (and proud of it)

To the editor:

Why is our Playboy Prime Minister attending parties, eating canapes and throwing back expensive wine, no doubt, when the rest of us, thanks to price and wage controls, are lucky to get a dry biscuit and a glass of Freshie on our night out?

If Trudeau wants us to tighten our belts, let him set the example, and that goes for his wife, who was too young for him in the first place, too.

Working Mother

To the editor:

It's too bad the victims of the murderers who languish in our jails because Trudeau lacks the guts to hang them aren't able to hear our PM's "Hello."

Capital Punishment Supporter

To the editor:

Perhaps we should look on the bright side of Trudeau's unfortunate "Hello" speech at a recent Ottawa reception. As long as he's saying "Hello" in Ottawa, he's not going around the world establishing friendly relations with the Japanese, the Cubans, the Chinese, the Russians, the Mexicans, the Germans or somebody else we haven't forgiven for a previous war, an ideology, the funny way they cook food, etc.

Almost Two Generations a Canadian

To the editor:

It's a good thing Prime Minister Trudeau said "Hello" to the visitor's face. If he had relied on his post office department,

Trudeau's message still wouldn't be there.

Ex-Trudeaumaniac

To the editor:

Trudeau's offhanded "Hello" is typical. No visitor to this country would be subjected to such uncalled-for familiarity if John Diefenbaker were still in charge. Undoubtedly our illustrious PM has taken us just one more step down the road to republicanism and a total break with Queen and Commonwealth.

On behalf of all Canadians who were embarrassed by the remark, I'd like to apologize to our foreign visitor and assure him he'll get a different welcome when Joe Clark becomes prime minister.

Tory Blue

To the editor:

Please cancel my subscription. I do not want a newspaper in my house that comes right out and quotes the Prime Minister as saying "Hello" to a guest of this country. Surely it would have been sufficient to report Mr. Trudeau said " . . ." to the visitor, and leave the rest to your readers' imaginations. For heaven's sake, some of us have children.

Old Subscriber

November 2, 1976

Chapter 7:
The World Stage

Pierre, eat peanuts at
the White House

PRIME MINISTER Trudeau leaves for Washington in a few days to speak to Congress and, if I'm any judge of Ottawa bureaucracy, he's already been given a list of do's and don'ts for the trip.

The instructions probably read like this:

If a man in a cardigan sweater greets you at the White House door, do not hand him your coat and hat. Chances are, it's the president.

Do not look directly at President Carter's face when he welcomes you as first exposure to his smile could cause temporary snowblindness.

To conserve energy, the thermostat in the White House has been set between 50 and 60°(F) therefore:

(a) Wear a fleece-lined cummerbund, thermal morning coat and electric dress socks to any formal talks scheduled for the Oval Office.

(b) Hold snow against the president's ear if it turns white during the course of important negotiations.

(c) Do not sign any trade agreements, friendship treaties, etc. without first blowing on your hands to get the circulation going.

(d) Try not to let your nose drip on the documents.

(e) Inform Mrs. Trudeau that the best thing to wear under her ball gown at a White House dinner would be a pair of off-the-shoulder Stanfields.

(f) Control the temptation to make a joke about President Carter keeping the White House so cold because it makes it easier for him to walk on water.

Eat peanuts at the White House reception.

If a lull develops in the conversation with Rosalynn, suggested topics for a chat include:

(a) How did Betty Ford leave the White House? Was she a good housekeeper?

(b) What is Barbara Walters really like?

(c) Did the president mentally cancel his subscription to Playboy magazine after they published his interview?

(d) Are Carter's Little Liver Pills any relation?

(e) Do they still get calls at the White House for R. Nixon?

Take along some gifts for the Carters—maple sugar candy for Amy Carter, an Eskimo carving for Mrs. Carter, an Indian sweater from B.C. for Jimmy Carter and a 6-pack of Labatt's 50 for Jimmy's brother, Billy.

Point out you rooted for the south in Gone With The Wind and the Atlanta Flames the last time they were at Maple Leaf Gardens.

Praise art work on the White House refrigerator as it's probably something brought home from school by Amy Carter.

Do not panic if Carter suggests eating grits. He's not offering Eugene Whelan in a 350 oven with a few potatoes tucked under his arms; he's talking about another unpalatable dish that's taken with a grain of salt, too.

Follow the first rule of international statesmanship: Never straighten to attention under a helicopter's blades, even if the White House band is playing your national anthem.

Do not accept a ride to Washington airport from Teddy Kennedy or Wilbur Mills.

Do not accept a ride to Ottawa airport from Jean Marchand or Rene Levesque.

Remember to pack a toothbrush and drink bottled water.

And have fun. End of briefing.

February 18, 1977

It's our duty to live beyond our means

PRIME MINISTER Trudeau can complain about the CBC, over-educated youth, Rene, reporters who pry into his personal life, grasping bankers and hundreds of other things.

However, when he criticizes Canadians for living beyond their means, he's going too far.

Living beyond one's means is as Canadian as maple syrup, ice hockey, or breathing. It's part of our way of life, and Prime Minister Trudeau has no business butting in.

Is there any Canadian in this vast land so lacking in spirit that he or she is content to live within the confines of the weekly pay check? Of course not. What a dull life that would be.

For heaven's sake, when I got out of college one of the things I wanted more than anything else in the world was a yellow sports car.

Did I have the income to justify it?

Don't be silly.

The only question was, would I buy the $3,000 sports car I couldn't afford, or would I be more sensible and go for the $2,400 model I couldn't afford either.

I settled for the more modest set of wheels (a 1954 MG-TF) and never looked back.

Since then I have been in hock constantly for cars, houses, major household appliances, posh vacations to places I had no right being.

What better incentive is there for a person to get ahead in the world than crushing debt?

If I hadn't been up to my hips in red ink, would I have stayed at the 9-to-5, would I have taken on extra jobs, would I have bothered to learn to spell and put in commas, some of them in the right places? Would I have kept out of trouble, more or less, and been a good boy?

Not very likely.

If I hadn't had this overwhelming desire to live over my head, to eat filet when the pay stub was shouting "wienies!" in my ear, undoubtedly I'd still be sleeping in 'til noon, and so would you.

How else do you make progress if you don't bite off more than you can chew and then scramble to catch up?

Gosh, a man's reach must exceed his grasp, or what's a bank loan for?

Perhaps some people reach that unfortunate state in life when their income matches their outgo, and they get fat and lazy and bored as a result.

But most of us, happily for the nation, are kept lean and hungry by mortgage payments, heating bills, $35 shoes for little Willy, and a new boat that sleeps four, or would if you didn't toss and turn all night wondering how you'll pay for it.

Hi, ho, that's the Canadian way.

If I dropped dead tomorrow, I wouldn't have time to attend the funeral because I have to work until I'm 77 to pay off our house. A 15-minute coffeebreak is all I can allow for the services, including glowing eulogy.

However, if Trudeau is really serious about us living within our means, I can offer only one suggestion: Cancel the income tax this year.

If Canadians didn't have to send so much money to Ottawa, many of us probably could make ends meet.

Over to you, Pierre.

March 30, 1977

Here's the sequel to Cinderella's story

A QUESTION that has bothered untold generations is, what happened to Cinderella afterward?

What took place after she put on the glass slipper and rode off into the sunset with Prince Charming?

Many theories have been advanced, but a friend of mine named Ray feels she has the true story of what transpired in the years that followed.

According to Ray, Cinderella and Prince Charming were married in a quiet ceremony that culminated their whirlwind courtship and made page one in every newspaper in the land.

No heart was so hardened that it wasn't touched by the romance of the moment and the photographs of the happy couple holding hands.

As befitting her new status, Cinderella moved into Prince Charming's big castle where she was waited on hand and foot and enjoyed every material comfort possible.

She had loads of servants, color TV, somebody to drive her wherever she wanted to go, an indoor swimming pool, no financial worries when she went shopping, and the affection of the entire nation.

99

However, Prince Charming spent a lot of time at the office because he was an important man and had to attend official dinners, make speeches, open buildings, confer with people a lot older than Cinderella, and take telephone calls even during the weekend.

Cinderella didn't enjoy such things and wanted Prince Charming to spend more time around the castle rather than traipsing off all over the place on business.

Alas, Prince Charming told Cinderella that it was part of the job and he didn't have time to dance every night. Even when Cinderella pointed out the thick layer of dust on her glass slippers, Prince Charming was firm. Life couldn't be one long ball, he stated.

In my friend Ray's version, Cinderella's discontentment grew in the months that followed, and even having a baby, then another, and then a third, didn't cheer her up.

If anything, Cinderella grew more depressed and stated more emphatically than ever that life in the castle wasn't all it was cracked up to be.

It might be romantic on the surface, she confided to almost everyone, but it was a real drag.

She didn't have a life of her own and, in dark moments, was sorry she ever asked the good fairy to turn the six white mice into fine horses and the pumpkin into a wonderful coach so she could go to that ball that seemed so long ago now.

To put in time and forget her boredom, Cinderella took up photography as a hobby, wrote poetry, snuck off from the castle for a few days on her own, and gave outrageous interviews about her life to the annoyance of Prince Charming.

Finally, in a fit of anger, she took her glass slippers out of the box where she kept them as a remembrance of her single days, and tossed them at Prince Charming.

"I'm through at the castle, and you can keep your glass slippers," she stated in a voice loud enough to be heard throughout the land.

And she stormed off, disappearing from sight while Prince Charming pondered what his next move would be.

Well, that's my friend Ray's story, and she claims it's true.

Sad, isn't it.

March 31, 1977

That was no face-lift, just a lift in spirits

EVER SINCE Prime Minister Trudeau showed up at his office with bandages under his eyes (and behind his ears, according to a Conservative spy), Canadians have been speculating whether he's had a facelift.

Are we going to wake up one morning and find the old familiar face gone from 24 Sussex Drive and, in its place, one that looks an awful lot like Moses or Winston Churchill?

Or will a new Charles de Gaulle rise up from the pile of surgical dressings and ride triumphant through cheering Quebec streets, too formidable a foe for Rene Levesque and his referendum?

Maybe Mr. Trudeau intends to give Joe Clark and Ed Broadbent the new face they're demanding at the nation's helm.

However, the PM's office claims Mr. Trudeau has not had a facelift, and we must take the spokesman at his word.

What, then, is the story behind the mysterious adhesive strips?

Here, for the first time anywhere, I am able to reveal that the nation's leader didn't, indeed, have a facelift. What took place was this:

The Prime Minister was busy at his desk a few days ago when an aide walked in with the latest Gallup poll figures.

"Would you like to see them?" the aide asked with the customary politeness.

In that split second Mr. Trudeau thought over the record of his administration—nearly a million unemployed, serious inflation, an RCMP scandal to contend with, the CANDU reactor fiasco, Quebec separation, high taxes, inept postal service, low morale in the armed forces, John Turner's defection, Otto Lang's use of government aircraft.

He also thought about his highly publicized marital breakup, his recent comment about all white Rhodesians being "racists;" he pondered the cabinet confrontations with James Richardson, Bryce Mackasey and Eric Kierans; he recalled the Bonaventure, the flip-flop on price and wage controls, the Company of Young Canadians.

The Prime Minister thought about it all—business stagnation, high mortgages, the outbursts of profanity, patronage.

Finally, biting his lip, Mr. Trudeau said, "All right, give me the Gallup poll results."

And he sat back, ready to wince.

"The Gallup poll indicates 51 per cent of Canadians would vote for you if an election were called today," the aide said.

Mr. Trudeau couldn't believe his ears.

In fact, he was so surprised his eyebrows shot up, up, and up and didn't come to a stop until they reached the top of the PM's head where they had no place else to go.

Try as they might, members of Trudeau's staff couldn't get his eyebrows down. Every time they edged them even an inch, they'd shoot back up again when Trudeau thought about the Gallup poll results.

Finally, a team of surgeons was summoned and they were able to return Mr. Trudeau's eyebrows to their normal position and hold them there with tape.

Facelifts are common, but what we've witnessed is the world's first face-lower.

Otherwise Mr. Trudeau would be walking around with the same look of astonishment on his face as millions of other Canadians.

July 19, 1977

Was Maggie discussing Pierre with Barbra?

THERE ARE some conversations a reporter would pay to overhear, and such a dialogue took place this week in New York City.

Prime Minister Trudeau's estranged wife Margaret and one of his old flames, Barbra Streisand, met at a party and, according to press reports, "spent hours in head-to-head conversation."

Perhaps they were only discussing the weather, the New York Yankees or setting a date for a photography session in Margaret's studio.

But it's more likely they were comparing notes on Mr. Trudeau.

Unfortunately, no transcript of their chat is available, so I've been forced to make one up. What did Maggie and Barbra have to say to each other? I suspect it went like this:

"Margaret, maybe a disco with hundreds of people around isn't the best place to ask, but I've been dying to find out about Pierre. How's his foreign policy? Does he have a good grasp on domestic developments? Is his majority . . . "

"Barbra, Barbra! One question at a time. First, Pierre is on good terms with the Soviet Union, the United States, and China."

"What a relief! I don't mind telling you I was worried about his international affairs."

"Before you get too excited, I should mention things aren't so good at home. I think it's safe to say he has very serious domestic problems on his hands."

"Do you mean . . . "

"Yes, the dollar has dipped to around 90 cents, unemployment is at the million mark, and Quebec is flirting with separatism."

"I'm sorry to hear it. Of course I only dated Pierre a short time but nothing he said to me indicated he was going to have trouble with the nation's economy. It just proves, I suppose, that you never know a man as well as you think."

"What did you talk about when you were dating Pierre, Barbra?"

"Oh, the usual things—freight rates, regional disparity, pollution threats to the fragile north, rights of native people, energy reserves in the 1980s."

"Isn't Pierre marvellous when he's in the mood for serious discourse? I don't know how many Saturday nights we sat around discussing Saskatchewan in the most intimate terms."

"Margaret, take it from me, you can count on one hand the number of men who can give you potash production figures off the top of his head over candlelight and wine, and tickle you with auto pact statistics."

"Barbra, we belong to a pretty exclusive group—the women who have watched great decisions being made and history rewritten. Most people have never met a philosopher-king let alone gone out with one."

"That's true. I remember Pierre promised if I came back to Ottawa for another visit, he'd introduce me to Mitchell Sharp and, if possible, let me discuss wheat prices with Otto Lang and egg marketing boards with Eugene Whelan. Sometimes I kick myself that I let it all slip through my fingers."

"Barbra, I know how you feel. It isn't easy to turn your back on winter in Ottawa, those lazy walks through the Senate, the excitement of having a deputy minister for dinner, the happy hours of listening to a CBC president regaling a few friends with amusing anecdotes about cable TV.

"Instead of being here, doing the Bump, I could be in Ottawa discovering what Rene Levesque is really like, or watching Pierre pore over reports from the finance ministry.

"But we have our careers to think about. All good things must end. Just be thankful we once had Camelot."

"I suppose you're right, Margaret. By the way, does Pierre still have that mole on his back?"

October 21, 1977

But Pierre, the bank wants cash

PRIME MINISTER Pierre Trudeau has instructed Canadians to solve their economic problems by thinking positively.

I've decided to take his advice.

Yesterday the usual flock of bills came in the mail but, instead of worrying about them or writing out a lot of checks, I threw them in the wastepaper basket and thought positively.

Unfortunately, Mr. Trudeau hasn't told us how much positive thought equals a dollar, but I thought positively for almost 20 minutes, figuring that should cover the full amount.

That problem solved, I then walked to work.

On the way to the office I passed at least three shabbily dressed men who were bumming quarters on street corners for cheap wine.

Rather than give them money, I told them they could solve their problems if they would only devote a small portion of each day to positive thinking.

If they thought positively long enough, I suggested, they would never have to panhandle again.

As luck would have it, the deep thought I offered seemed beyond their mental grasp for they returned my words with vicious oaths muttered through blue lips.

Ordinarily I send out our mortgage payment on the house on the 23rd of each month but, warming to our PM's new approach to fiscal ills, I sent the bank a letter.

"In lieu of actual cash, I will think positively about the December payment for one hour and 30 minutes between now and the January instalment," I promised.

I mailed the letter without a postage stamp, but with a flash of positive thought, enough to cover the 12 cents postage.

By the middle of the day, I could see the wisdom of Mr. Trudeau's way of doing things. I had taken care of all sorts of debts and not once reached in my pocket for any cash.

Because I'm rather good at positive thinking, I soon arrived at the idea that we could probably double our standard of living now that positive thinking had replaced money.

My wife could think positively about the groceries, the electric bill, the telephone charges and the gas company. That would leave me to think positively about the house, the car, the clothing and recreation expenses.

And that would still leave us three children to do positive thinking.

Besides clothing themselves, so I decided, there's no reason why they couldn't do an extra 15 minutes of deep thought every day and put away something for an annual vacation.

To be on the safe side, I didn't include the positive thinking of our dog in the monthly budget because, even though she has an intelligent face, I don't think a family should depend on the dog to carry its own share. That would be a little naive.

Frankly, everything went extremely well under Prime Minister Trudeau's system until supper time.

We sent out for some Chinese food for dinner and, when the delivery man came, he handed me the bill.

I looked at it and offered him the equivalent in positive thinking plus what I considered a generous tip, all told about eight solid minutes of positive thinking.

Unfortunately, the delivery man hadn't heard of Prime Minister Trudeau's remedy for putting the economy right and wanted cash.

It has struck me that only one or two people who insist on doing business the old way could upset Prime Minister Trudeau's apple-cart, and mine.

December 21, 1977

What is Pierre's secret of youth?

CANADIANS have been rubbing their eyes ever since the Liberal convention in Ottawa last weekend. Frankly, they still can't believe what they saw.

There in all the newspapers are photographs of Prime Minister Pierre Trudeau, delivering speeches, shaking hands, greeting the party faithful, smiling at the cheering masses.

That in itself is not unusual.

The amazing thing is Trudeau looks exactly the way he did in 1968, when he swept to power on a wave of Trudeaumania.

Gone are the high forehead, graying temples, and flowing locks of just a few months ago when if the wind was blowing, he looked like a Mercedes sports coupe with the doors open.

Absent, too, is the 1973 Trudeau when he resembled Sir John A. Macdonald, hair over his collar, ears hidden in the regal sideburns.

No, what we have in 1978 is a clean-cut carbon copy of the Trudeau of 10 years ago, and if you don't believe me, examine the photographs.

How did the Liberals manage to rejuvenate their leader?

Has Senator Keith Davey hired a team of scientists who, through the miracle of cloning, have produced a new, younger Trudeau by scraping a few cells from the pinkie of the old model?

By some mysterious deal with the Devil, is there now an oil portrait in the attic at 24 Sussex Dr. that is growing older and more wrinkled by the minute while our Pierre defies the ravages of time?

Is that really an imposter standing up there, flashing his teeth at the news photographers, a Rich Little, perhaps, or a Craig Russell?

Or has Trudeau been whisked off to some Swiss clinic where a new set of glands has been installed in his innards, organs that guarantee a lifespan of 200 years of normal use, provided he brings them in every six months for a grease and lube and keeps his rad topped up?

For all I know, the Trudeau we saw over the weekend may be a stuffed figure operated by remote control from a back room where Liberal brain-trusters take turns on the microphone. A sort of Grit Artoo-Deetoo.

But it is baffling.

Certainly the rest of us have aged plenty since Trudeau took office. Does he know something you and I, and Ponce de Leon, don't?

Whatever the answer to the nation's most puzzling mystery, the strategy of the Liberal party in the next election is now crystal clear:

If they have a 1968 Trudeau model on their hands, obviously they'll run a 1968-style campaign with loads of kisses, bright promises, and sunny faces.

While Trudeau has been rejuvenated, Joe Clark has been trying desperately to look as old as possible. He doesn't think the Boy Scout image he now projects will attract votes.

So he's attempting to look like Bob Stanfield, or John Diefenbaker, while Trudeau . . .

1968, here we come.

March 1, 1978

Put Pierre where he belongs—abroad

THOUSANDS of Canadians have wondered why Prime Minister Trudeau hasn't done a better job of running the country.

After watching his performances at the United Nations and at the NATO meetings, I may have the answer: His present job isn't big enough for him.

No, I'm not kidding.

Whenever Mr. Trudeau steps on the world stage, he's at his absolute best—addressing Congress, conferring with the Callaghans, Carters and Brezhnevs, visiting distant lands on official business.

Everyone falls in love with him and his speeches positively brim with good sense, wit and clarity.

Is this the same person we see in question period, thumping his desk and shouting coarsely across the aisle at Sinc, Gloomy Ed, Dief and the rest? Is this the philosopher-king from the land of 900,000 unemployed, the 88-cent dollar and rampant separatism?

No, it is a different Trudeau, one who checks his fuddle-duddles in a locker at Ottawa airport before leaving for Washington, Paris, Moscow, etc.

In a way, the Trudeau phenomenon is understandable. We all know accountants who can run large corporations but are shaky on their eight-times table. There are doctors who can do a lovely job on a gall bladder, but need their wives' help when trying to carve the Sunday joint.

And it is not unusual for a university professor to win some global award for his text on 12th century Chinese philosophy and then not remember where he left his car after he leaves the dinner.

Mr. Trudeau, I submit, falls in that category.

He does not understand Medicine Hat, or why wage and profit restraints are ignored by labor and business, but consider his plusses as a world leader:

(1) He speaks several languages, a problem if singing a national anthem at a Canadian sports event but a distinct advantage in international affairs when you're trying to make a point about

the neutron bomb or missile production;

(2) He has travelled the world and knows not to ask for ketchup when served a goat's eye, and when to wear the good socks because the hostess expects you to take off your shoes for dinner;

(3) He is single, sort of, and therefore a tempting prospect for sheiks, presidents, kings, commissars and the like who have an extra place at the table and an unmarried sister-in-law or cousin who giggles a lot;

(4) Even though he is nearing 60, he is in superb physical condition and can probably outrun, out-trampoline, out-party, outswim and out anything else any leader currently on the world scene, not an unimportant bonus.

With that in mind, it would seem obvious that the larger setting of the world should be Mr. Trudeau's new lifework—secretary general of the UN, perhaps, when Waldheim's term is up, or ambassador at large for the Western powers.

Yes, a Kissinger with a boutonniere.

Off the top of my head, I can't think of a nation in the world, outside of Canada, where Mr. Trudeau isn't popular and where he doesn't shine.

So why not start a fund to take Mr. Trudeau out of Ottawa and into the big league of world politics?

It's only a guess but I bet John Turner would be willing to serve as campaign chairman and throw the first $100 into the pot.

June 2, 1978

Pierre lifts a finger, Canada's letters editors cower

NO ONE was more dismayed by Prime Minister Trudeau's obscene gesture to the press photographers at the Bonn summit than editors of the nation's letters-to-the-editor pages.

Like the rest of us, these hardworking men and women like to taper off during the summer months, fill up their columns with whimsical notes about the Canadian postal service and get home early.

And who can blame them?

However, with one sudden lift of his arm, Mr Trudeau has spoiled the dream of quiet contemplation and a quick swing on the backyard hammock before digging into the barbecued wienies.

Even as these words are being tapped out, thousands of irate citizens across the land are hunched over their Big Boy scribblers, dashing off hot notes to the local daily in protest over the PM's behavior on the world stage.

If you put an ear to the ground you can hear them grinding their teeth, and thumbing furiously through Roget's Thesaurus for the alternates to "disgusting."

An estimated 2,500 letters will apologize on behalf of all Canadians to the rest of the world for Mr. Trudeau's "uncalled-for" behavior.

Another 3,000 to 4,000 will ask Canadians if they need any more proof that this man is unfit to lead the nation.

A minimum of 4,500 will reflect gloomily on how the quality of leadership has degenerated and how, for the first time in over 20 years, the writers conclude they must vote Conservative in the next federal election.

At least 7 will chide Canadians for not having a sense of humor and realizing that the PM was merely pulling the leg of reporters.

There could be as many as 10,000 letters from subscribers who want it publicly known that nothing Mr. Trudeau does surprises them anymore and the same goes for Margaret.

Add in letters from people who (a) claim they're tired of reading about Mr. Trudeau, (b) see in the upraised arm another plot to turn Canada into a republic, (c) want to chide the newspapers for exposing readers to such trash when the space could be better used for an in-depth analysis of the proposed constitution, or soccer scores from Albania, (d) think the PM might have a trick elbow and should see a reputable chiropractor.

And it will all land on the Opinion Page desk.

Instead of going fishing on some sun-splashed northern lake, musing over deep questions of a philosophical nature at a Bertrand Russell symposium, or just quietly getting hammered at the Press Club bar, the person handling the letters will be up to his copy pencil in comment about the PM's "international gesture of disdain" as one writer delicately put it.

What a cruel blow it is.

Mr. Trudeau can wiggle his fingers and then take off for a European holiday, but he leaves in his wake all those people who now must put headings on the bales of letters from reacting Canadians.

I'd say the PM should write a personal note of apology to every letters-to-the-editor department head in the country for screwing up their summer.

But the poor devils probably have enough mail pouring in without one more from him to contend with.

July 19, 1978

Tories love Trudeau but Grits need Joe

MY FAVORITE contact, Irate Reader, has an interesting assessment of the coming elections.

The way he sees it, the biggest asset the Liberals feel they have going for them is Joe Clark, and the biggest asset the Conservatives feel they have going for them is Pierre Trudeau.

Each party is counting on the other party's leader to sweep it into power, and with a majority.

"At this point in the campaign, the Liberals are almost totally dependent on Joe Clark for votes, and the Conservatives are counting just as heavily on Pierre Trudeau to produce the kind of momentum they need to take over the government," he said. "It's a unique situation."

"Don't the Liberals feel they can win without the help of Joe Clark?" I wanted to know.

"Even Senator Keith Davey isn't that optimistic. Sinc Stevens, Dief, Otto Jelinek and Tom Cossitt may produce some votes for the Liberals, but the key is Clark. If he comes through for them as the Liberals expect, they'll remain in charge."

"What has Clark done for the Liberals so far?"

"He's gift-wrapped Quebec for them, but that's all any one can say for certain. Meanwhile, Trudeau has all but presented Alberta, Manitoba and Nova Scotia to the Tories on a platter."

"Trudeau has had some help from Otto Lang, Francis Fox, Jean Goyer and Jean Chretien," I insisted. "He didn't make it single-handed."

"True," Irate Reader admitted, "it was a team effort, but he is the focal point of the Conservative swing in the opinion polls.

"As I see it, the next election will be decided in Ontario. It could plop in the lap of the Tories, thanks to Trudeau's efforts, or it could take another Liberal leap because of Clark."

"It must be nerve-wracking for a political party to rely so completely on another party leader's efforts for their success," I suggested. "After all, the Liberals have no control over Clark, and the same goes for the Conservatives and Trudeau, yet their fates hang in the balance."

"The Conservatives are confident Trudeau will pull it off for them," he responded, "and the Liberals are just as convinced that, if there is a way for a Grit victory, Clark will find it."

"So what will the parties' strategy be between now and election day?"

"The Liberals want Joe Clark to get as much media coverage as possible, for him to put his ideas on record, to have his picture taken, and to appear on as many radio open-line shows as he can squeeze in. Given enough exposure, they're convinced Clark can only be an asset to the Liberal party.

"On the other hand, the Conservatives have exactly the same idea about Trudeau. They feel there are two kinds of people in Canada, those who vote Conservative, and those who haven't been convinced yet by Trudeau."

"There are still lots of undecided voters in Canada, probably hundreds of thousands," I pointed out.

"Don't worry, by election day every Canadian will have made up his mind which leader to vote against," he said.

October 11, 1978

If PM is defeated, what will Trudeau-haters do?

AT A TIME in our history when jobs are already scarce enough, it appears Canada could be on the verge of losing yet another major industry—the anti-Trudeau industry.

In the past 11 years, the anti-Trudeau industry has grown until now it is big business. In fact, at this moment there are thousands of Canadians who criticize Prime Minister Trudeau for a living.

And I'm not talking about amateurs and dabblers.

I'm talking about professionals—editorial writers, newspaper cartoonists, media commentators with open line shows, after-dinner speakers, labor leaders, representative of large and small corporations, politicians.

Well, the list could go on.

What's to become of them if, as many experts now are predicting, Prime Minister Trudeau is defeated in the next federal election, possibly next spring?

Who will they take swipes at with pen and throat for the daily bread, who will they blame (for a $350 fee) for the nation's ills after the Eskimo log dessert and 10-minute introduction, who will they scorch in hot paragraphs in an attempt to pay off the condominium's 11 per cent mortgage?

And it's not just the visible Trudeau critic whose professional fate, and youngster's orthopedic work, hang in the balance.

There are dozens of spinoffs in the anti-Trudeau industry:

Researchers required to look up embarrassing quotes from 1968 Trudeau speeches; factory workers to turn out grease pencils for the vicious Trudeau caricatures; photographers for the bad angle snapshots of Trudeau that can be played on page one beside the searing editorial; clerks in shops that rent formal attire to $100-a-plate Trudeau roasts; anti-Trudeau bumper sticker designers; stenographers to remind members of the anti-Trudeau rally Wednesday.

Those, and many more, depend heavily on what has become Canada's fastest growing industry to keep the world from the door and pay the Chargex on last spring's trip to Mexico.

113

If Trudeau goes, so will the entire industry. What happens then to George and Peter and Dennis and Dunc and Doug and Charlie and Al and Richard and Lubor and...

Well, what happens to them all?

Will they be forced to stand on drafty streetcorners, wind whistling through threadbare camel hair, last year's Dacks on tired feet, tin cup of cheap ballpoint pens in extended hand, and fighting off the cymbal-clanging Hare Krishna for the next pedestrian to come their way?

Will our Mr. Bain's next book, because of reduced circumstances, be Cooking Sherry Is For Breakfast?

To fill the vacancy left by the Trudeau Must Go editorials, will the Toronto Sun be forced to run news or, even worse, pictures of fully clothed women?

Will Dalton Camp, gasp, turn in his quill and apply for a number in the Manpower line?

Alas, it could all come to pass.

Unfortunately, it is a Canadian characteristic to wait until the last moment to take action but, with so many jobs on the line, we can't sit back and wait for disaster to strike.

Sure, the anti-Trudeau industry has been a boom to the economy. Yes, we're all grateful for the benefits it's brought.

But let's act now.

Let's re-tool and get an early start on an anti-Joe Clark industry. It may not take up all the slack, not at first, but at least it's something.

October 16, 1978

Can Begin bring peace to Canada?

ISRAELI Prime Minister Menachem Begin is coming to Canada Nov. 6 on what has been billed as a "goodwill" tour of Ottawa, Montreal and Toronto.

According to the news report, he'll make some speeches, attend luncheons and confer with various groups of Israeli supporters in Canada.

However, the suspicion is growing that the real purpose of the Begin trip is to arrange a peace treaty between Pierre Trudeau and John Turner.

Ever since the two men broke off diplomatic relations and Mr. Turner resigned from the Trudeau cabinet, the Liberal party has been torn with strife and it is thought that Mr. Begin is the one man who might be able to heal the breach.

According to this theory, the Israeli Prime Minister will invite the two leading Liberals to some neutral ground where he will explain to them that they may both go down the tubes if they don't resolve their differences.

Mr. Begin is expected to point out for starters how much they have in common and how it is in their mutual interest to bury the hatchet once and for all.

If they can come to some sort of agreement, the Israeli leader will say, there is no reason why Liberals from sea to sea can't live in harmony again and raise their little ones in an atmosphere without tension and distrust.

Although it can't be confirmed, the differences between the two Liberals are large but not insurmountable.

Mr. Trudeau, so it is claimed, feels Mr. Turner should never have written those newsletters to leading businessmen in which he gave candid and not flattering assessments of the Liberal cabinet. Mr. Trudeau is also reported disenchanted over Mr. Turner's resignation from office just when the going got rough.

On the other hand, Mr. Turner was put out by Mr. Trudeau's cold treatment of him at the personal level and the apparent lack of opportunity for advancement in his administration.

How will Mr. Begin approach these difficult negotiations and heal the breach?

Apparently the Begin peace plan depends on Mr. Turner publicly embracing Mr. Trudeau and accepting an invitation to return to the Liberal party as No. 2 man.

In return Mr. Trudeau would promise to withdraw from 24 Sussex Dr. and agree to do everything in his power to ensure that Mr. Turner would eventually take over the premises.

One time schedule would have Mr. Turner and Mr. Trudeau fighting the federal election next spring, side by side, and then

Mr. Trudeau stepping down a year to 18 months later, having placed his endorsing hand on Mr. Turner's shoulder.

As I said at the start, it's all speculation up 'til now but observers say we shouldn't be surprised if we turn on our television sets some evening to be confronted by a special news program in which Mr. Turner and Mr. Trudeau will hug each other, with a smiling Mr. Begin in between.

If Mr. Begin can pull this one off, it will mean a Nobel Peace Prize for him, not to mention a sound night's sleep for Sen. Keith Davey.

October 23, 1978

Chapter 8: Interruption

Trudeau on Toronto has us speechless

MEMBERS of the Toronto media are still seething over a remark Prime Minister Trudeau made Monday at a Liberal fund-raising dinner in the city. Some are even prepared to go on record as stating that it was definitely hitting below the belt.

What the PM said, and there are 2,000 witnesses who will swear to it, was: "Toronto is the best city in Canada."

Those are his exact words, and not out of context.

Probably no seven words ever uttered by Mr. Trudeau have caused so much concern among senior editors, columnists, radio and TV analysts, editorial writers and other serious commentators on the Canadian scene.

In recent years journalists have attacked all of the Prime Minister's speeches and torn them apart, word for word, practically syllable for syllable.

But no one in the Toronto media had been able to find a flaw in his "Toronto is the best city in Canada" statement, and it's now 48 hours later.

Being unable to criticize a Trudeau speech is driving Toronto newsmen nuts.

If he had said something as mildly controversial as "Merry Christmas," we could have worked in some reference to unemployment figures, the Bryce Mackasey appointment, or three or four snide remarks about Christmas being merrier if John Turner were in charge.

But "Toronto is the best city in Canada"?

What can we blast there?

After talking it over with several of my colleagues, we've come to the conclusion that Mr. Trudeau included that sentence deliberately, knowing full well the consternation it would cause among journalists.

"There can be no other explanation," one in-depth commentator charged with an edge of bitterness in his voice.

"He knew before he started if he said 'Toronto is the best city in Canada,' we wouldn't have a comeback, that we'd have to sit back and take it without so much as an 'Oh, yeah!'

"I can't remember ever being so frustrated by a Trudeau speech, either formal or off-the-cuff."

"Do you think the unfortunate comment was written for him by Senator Keith Davey, Jim Coutts or one of his other aides?" I asked, seeking to pinpoint blame.

My fellow journalist said he didn't think so.

"It's so fiendishly clever I'm positive it's the work of the Prime Minister himself. If he had only added 'I believe' to the front of 'Toronto is the best city in Canada,' we could have nailed him.

"We could have ripped him apart for not being absolutely sure Toronto is the best city in Canada, and then tossed in some unflattering statistics about Canada's balance of trade deficit and mentioned in passing how little we also think of Margaret Trudeau's latest film.

"But he didn't leave us so much as a scrap to get indignant over."

"I'm almost certain 'Toronto is the best city in Canada' won't go down very well in Montreal, Vancouver, Winnipeg, London, Calgary and dozens of other places," I commented. "The media there will take a strip off the PM's back for his statement."

"That's still not going to help us in Toronto," the editor moaned. "Let's face it, we've been had."

December 20, 1978

Help poor Pierre:
Get a unity tattoo

A "HUMBLED" Prime Minister Trudeau was in Toronto this week and, according to press reports, he admitted he was in "trouble" and needed the "help" of Canadians.

Naturally, we all want to do what we can to help our leader, but there may be some people who aren't sure what assistance the PM has in mind.

Fortunately, I have been able to put together a few ways we can give Mr. Trudeau a helping hand.

119

1. Take Air Canada the next time you go on a trip and, when you get home, send a nice note to Bryce Mackasey telling him what a wonderful job he's doing as chairman of the air line.

2. Tell a Joe Clark joke today. (Sample: Of course Maureen McTeer has a sense of humor. She married Joe Clark, didn't she?)

3. When Margaret Trudeau's revealing book is published this spring, organize a protest group and picket your nearest Coles outlet with placards that read, "Clubbing Prime Ministers is not sport."

4. Start a Jean Chretien fan club in your community.

5. Have "Sovereignty Association no, 10 Provinces In A Strong Federalist System yes" tatooed across some part of your anatomy that can be exposed in the summer months without violating a section of the Criminal Code or alienating an important religious group.

6. Suggest your child make an oleomargarine sculpture (life size) of Eugene Whelan for his or her school's next science fair.

7. Print up a batch of bumper stickers that say, "If you believe in Senator Keith Davey, honk" and distribute them to friends and loved ones.

8. Name your son's pet rat "Rene."

9. At the end of your shift at work, refrain from saying in a loud voice that carries, "Another day, another 83 cents."

10. At cocktail parties, service club luncheons, pep rallies for the school basketball team, etc., never let an opportunity slip to mention that the only thing the Conservatives promised in the last election was price and wage controls, and the Liberals proved they wouldn't work.

11. Purchase space in a newspaper and run a political ad that states, "Moses came out of the wilderness with the 10 Commandments; Joe Clark came out of the wilderness with Sinc Stevens."

12. Get a marker pencil and draw a moustache on any old photographs of Peter Lougheed you have lying around the house.

13. Save your very sternest look for any smart aleck who insists on referring to Otto Lang as The Flying Hun.

14. Make plans now to purchase enough tulip bulbs so you can do a nice floral outline of Governor-General Ed Schreyer's head in your garden this year.

15. Start a rumor in your community that John Diefenbaker is trying to legally change his first name to Ayatollah.

16. Get up a petition on your street demanding that the local television station give more TV coverage to Joe Clark, especially if he undertakes another world tour.

17. Refuse to buy any saucy posters of Francis Fox that show him in an unflattering light, or position.

18. Make out a new will in which you ask, in the event of death, that your most vital part—your vote—be given to a needy Liberal

If we all pull together, I'm sure we can get Mr. Trudeau out of his "trouble."

February 23, 1979

Wrong sometimes but often right

TRUDEAU did it right.

Tuesday night at home, around the dinner table, he told his three sons he had a big secret for them, and that they mustn't tell anyone.

He was quitting.

They were the first to know their father was leaving politics, the Liberal leadership, another chance at being Prime Minister.

And that is how it should have been. The kids knowing first.

Also, Trudeau quit for the right reasons.

He was plain tired. Tired of meetings, tired of arguments, tired of the shouts across the Commons floor, just tired.

Maybe the final proof for Trudeau was the weekend Liberal convention in Toronto. Four days of constant spotlight, four major speeches, four days of gladhanding, they left him weary.

The demands were more than he could cope with any more.

And he realized it.

But perhaps the real turning point in Trudeau's mind came a week earlier when he went to New York for a night on the town with somebody named Linda rather than to the meeting of the British Columbia Liberals.

Trudeau knew he should have been at the B.C. meeting; he

acknowledged the B.C. Liberals had every right to be sore.

The truth, though, was Trudeau would rather be discoing in New York with somebody named Linda than at another political meeting.

That's when he knew it was time to quit.

The work was no longer fun.

So Tuesday night he told his kids, and Wednesday morning he told the nation.

Privately he said he didn't have it any more—the hunger, that extra step, the old pizzazz. He didn't want to play "performing seal"; it was over.

When Trudeau went to the Liberal caucus Wednesday morning to tell them the news, the MPs were in the midst of discussing this week's by-elections. They finished and then Trudeau spoke.

He sat in his chair and read his retirement announcement and, before he could finish, choked up and stopped.

There was a pause and then the Trudeau wit saved the moment.

"You guys always knew underneath I was a softie," Trudeau said.

Afterward he went back to his office where a pumpkin carved by one of his sons for Hallowe'en still sits by the window.

Then came the press conference.

More emotion.

And than a lovely line borrowed, and flipped around, from an old Richard Nixon speech of 1962.

After paying tribute to the media, Trudeau admitted, "I'm sorry I won't have you guys to kick around any more."

A nice touch.

When asked what he was planning to do, Trudeau said he wanted to call Claude Ryan in the afternoon to talk about the referendum.

And then nothing special.

One of his closest aides, Senator Keith Davey, kidded Trudeau and said it was difficult to think of him as "an elder statesman." He also predicted the press would be filled with flattering stories in 24 hours.

He was right.

The burden of almost 11 years as Prime Minister has taken its toll and Trudeau, wrong sometimes but right often, has served us well.

122

It is not inappropriate at this moment to say a sincere "thanks."
And "merci."

November 22, 1979

Pierre? Pierre Who?

MANY CANADIANS are wondering whether Pierre Trudeau will be able to return to politics successfully after his 27-day retirement.

On Nov. 21, Mr. Trudeau announced he was leaving politics and it wasn't until noon of Dec. 18 that he revealed his intention to return to the political arena and lead the Liberal party in the Feb. 18 federal election.

"Will he be able to make the adjustment after being absent from the political scene for so long?" I asked an Ottawa contact.

"It won't be easy," my informant admitted. "When you've been out of the limelight and away from the pressures of politics for that length of time, there's a real danger a person can lose his touch. You forget just how demanding the job of leading a party can be."

"It would have been a lot easier if Mr. Trudeau hadn't waited so long on the sidelines," I suggested. "If he had announced his comeback at the beginning of December instead of so close to the end of the month, I'd be more optimistic about his chances."

"Exactly. It would even have been better from his point of view if he had made the re-entry into political life at 9 o'clock in the morning yesterday rather than three hours later. As it is, it could be touch and go."

"I suppose the Liberals will have some kind of plan to help their rusty leader get over the initial shock of being back in politics."

"Yes, Senator Keith Davey, Jim Coutts, Jean Chretien and others will undoubtedly give him a crash course on what has happened in Canadian politics during his absence and try to bring Mr. Trudeau up to date."

"I hope for his sake Mr. Trudeau is a fast learner."

"If he isn't, he'll be a dead duck. A lot of changes have taken place in those 27 days he's been out of action and Mr. Trudeau hasn't a moment to lose if he hopes to avoid making a fool of himself."

"Do you think the timing in his speeches will still be there and that his lengthy absence won't make him nervous when he faces a crowd for that first time?"

"It will be a traumatic experience, no doubt about that. You can't expect to come out of an extended retirement and not feel the effects. The Liberals, in fact, are taking quite a gamble in going with Mr. Trudeau when there are members of their party who don't have the liability of being on the shelf since last Nov. 21."

"Maybe the Liberals feel they can turn the drawback into an advantage," I responded. "They can tell the public they now have a leader who is well rested and fresh, someone who has had time to think about great issues and problems as a private citizen. He isn't tired out and scarred up like Joe Clark or Ed Broadbent."

"That's possible, but the Liberals also risk the criticism of having a leader who lacks recent experience in politics. There could be a backlash from people who say the country needs the firm hand of a leader who hasn't been on the sidelines so long."

"Predicting public reaction is pretty difficult," I said.

"That's right. Mr. Trudeau has been away from the Ottawa scene so long, there's probably a generation of Canadians who don't know who he is and will have to be brought up to date on his career.

"If the Liberals are wise, they'll send out a personality profile on Mr. Trudeau immediately so the country can get re-acquainted with him."

"I just hope Mr. Trudeau realizes what he's let himself in for," I said.

"Amen," my Ottawa source said. "I also hope the NDP and the Conservatives aren't too rough on him in the first weeks of the campaign."

"That's the best they can do until Mr. Trudeau gets back in the political swing and learns how to take care of himself again."

December 19, 1979

We're on the brink of a new shortage—the insult crisis

CANADA is in the middle of its second federal election campaign in nine months and, as a result, the politicians of this nation are running out of insults.

They've said just about every nasty thing they can think of about each other and are now facing a dangerous shortage of barbs, digs and brickbats.

Obviously, if somebody doesn't come up with some vicious one-liners fast, candidates in the Feb. 18 election may soon be forced to deliver speeches that don't contain a single derogatory reference to their opponents.

Can you imagine, for example, Prime Minister Clark standing in a packed auditorium unable to deliver a zinger about Mr. Trudeau? Or Mr. Broadbent (or Mr. Trudeau) starting a sentence like, "Prime Minister Clark is..." and then not having an appropriate, devastating finish?

It's too much to even contemplate.

Therefore, it's up to all of us to contribute whatever snotty lines we have to maintain the country's insult stockpile in our hour of need.

Here are a few modest suggestions the leaders can use in the current crisis:

Joe Clark operates with all the efficiency of a Toronto Argo game plan.

Ed Broadbent has been talking about oil and natural gas so often it's safe to say nobody in the country knows more than he does about hot air.

Pierre Trudeau thinks solving the unemployment problem means finding another $95,000 a year job for Bryce Mackasey.

I wouldn't say Joe Clark was inept but the other day he tried to put his foot in his mouth and missed.

Ed Broadbent thinks so much of poor people he wants every Canadian to become one.

The Liberals have a name for Pierre Trudeau's platform in this election. It's called the Old Deal.

Somebody has to stop Joe Clark before he gives mediocrity a bad name.

I wouldn't say Ed Broadbent has a high opinion of his own virtue but he's ordered two fishes and five loaves for the next NDP banquet.

Pierre Trudeau's idea of economy is driving last year's Mercedes.

Joe Clark is living proof life doesn't begin at 40.

Just because he's planning to change his name to Dennis McBroadbent is no reason to say the leader of the NDP is in the pocket of Big Labor.

Pierre Trudeau says the Ayatollah Khomeini is wrong when he claims to talk to God. Pierre has checked over his phone bills and there isn't any record of such calls being made.

Joe Clark knows he's offended some voters by backing off his promise to move the Canadian embassy to Jerusalem, so he's invited leaders of the Jewish community to the house Saturday night for a pork dinner.

Ed Broadbent feels with proper planning there's no reason why Canada couldn't be the Britain of tomorrow.

Of course Pierre Trudeau needs the Prime Minister's job. He's too old now to chase girls and too young to play for the Toronto Maple Leafs.

Joe Clark and Peter Lougheed have been asked to star in a movie based on the life of Edgar Bergen. You can guess which one will play Charlie McCarthy.

Ed Broadbent is the kind of guy who if he died and went to heaven would find something to complain about.

Pierre Trudeau says it's sheer nonsense to suggest he's cut off from the real world by advisers like Jim Coutts and Allan MacEachen, and that John Diefenbaker should be ashamed spreading such outrageous stories.

Did you hear they are naming a wine after Joe Clark? Dead Duck.

Ed Broadbent is the kind of person who would cut out the songs in The Sound of Music to speed up the story.

Why is everyone so mad at Pierre Trudeau in this campaign? After all, he hasn't said anything yet.

Well, I hope that holds them for awhile.

January 10, 1980

Here's what the parties say —now you can ignore them

CANDIDATES in the Feb. 18 election are busy making speeches, sending out brochures, giving in-depth interviews to the media and appearing in church halls and school gymnasiums from Victoria to St. John's.

And what are they thinking and saying?

To save you time, I've summarized the platforms of all the men and women seeking office, regardless of political party. Here is the result:

What are the candidates for? Human dignity, strong leadership, an economy that's moving again, important government spending cuts, a better standard of living for all Canadians, an end (once and for all) to regional disparities, fairer treatment of the Canadian Indian, development of the Canadian north, a government that will face problems head-on rather than sweep them under the carpet, more opportunities for young people, a bigger share of world markets for Canadian manufacturing, a society in which the farmer (laborer, newcomer, etc.) can hold his head high.

What are the candidates against? Government waste, unemployment (especially of the young), needlessly high energy costs, inflation, the Soviet invasion of Afghanistan, American control of our economy, clogged-up courts, Alberta's Heritage fund, the shabby way society treats the old, an administration in Ottawa that isn't responsive to the public, high interest rates, any breakup of the nation, powerful interest groups that put themselves before the good of the country, broken promises, land speculators, the cost of housing (especially for couples starting out), lack of direction in Ottawa.

Where do candidates feel is Canada's rightful place? In the forefront of the world, among the leaders of the free world, shoulder-to-shoulder with the great powers working toward peace in the world, and definitely not in the background.

Do candidates feel Canada's voice should be heard in Moscow, Washington and the other capitals of the world? Yes.

127

What do candidates feel Canada should be extending to the superpowers but also to Third World countries who are not as fortunate as we are? The hand of friendship.

Do candidates feel Canadians have a lot to be thankful for? Yes, we are among the most blessed people on the face of the earth and should get over the Canadian habit of grumbling and always looking on the gloomy side of things.

Why do candidates feel this is an important election? Because this is Canada's last chance to regain control of its own destiny, because this is the most critical election in the country's history, because time is running out on Canada, because the choice made on election day will affect our children for years, perhaps decades, to come.

How do candidates expect to win? In spite of the media.

What do candidates promise to do if elected? To do their best, to always have a door open for all people in their riding, to get on with the business of government, to speak out clearly on issues, to make this a better country in which to live, to start a newsletter to keep constituents better informed, to take a message to Ottawa ("We will not tolerate high prices any longer," "We want our fair share and we want it now" etc.) to be his own man, to stand up for the little guy.

Why are the candidates willing to offer themselves for public office? Because there's a job to be done, to guarantee a better world for children, to pay back Canada for all she has provided in the past, to make a fresh start for the country, and because it wouldn't be possible to look in the mirror mornings if they didn't come forward at this time.

And what do the candidates expect to say the day after election day? That the people have spoken.

Now you don't have to read any more election stories in the next month.

January 16, 1980

Oh for day when Joe Clark turns guns on Brezhnev

T HE SOVIET Union's invasion of Afghanistan has upset some Canadians who feel it's time Prime Minister Clark took off the kid gloves and gave Chairman Brezhnev a real tongue-lashing.

"Mr. Clark has already said some strong things," I pointed out in the Prime Minister's defence. "He's threatened economic sanctions and an Olympic boycott and promised not to replace grain shipments cut off by President Carter.

"How far do you want him to go?"

"I think he should pull out all the stops and treat Brezhnev the way he treats Trudeau," the hawk stated firmly.

"You mean accuse Brezhnev of the same things he's accusing Trudeau of in newspaper interviews, radio hotline shows and major campaign addresses?"

"Yes. In fact, all Mr. Clark would have to do is change Trudeau's name where it appears in the text of a speech to Brezhnev. The rest of the speech could be used word for word."

"Are you out of your mind?" I asked. "It's true the Soviet Union has invaded Afghanistan with 100,000 troops, executed the former leader of the country, established martial law, sent a few thousand tanks to the Iranian border and upset detente and the balance of power in the world, but is that any reason to subject Chairman Brezhnev to the kind of language Prime Minister Clark has heaped on Trudeau?"

"I feel that strongly about the Afghanistan invasion," was the terse reply.

"Strong enough to call Brezhnev arrogant, cynical, dishonest, leader of a bad government with a shameful record?"

"Yes."

"Even strong enough to say he can't be trusted, that he's a disaster, that he's too old, that he's chicken, that he manipulates people and is uncaring?"

"Yes."

"You really are outraged by the Soviet military offensive; I can see that now."

"I'd tell you how far I'd be willing to go," the hawk said. "I'd re-edit the commercials Prime Minister Clark's party is showing on television right now and substitute 'Brezhnev' wherever mention is made of Trudeau."

"If Mr. Clark did that, we'd all be digging bomb shelters in our basements by the end of the week. You can't say that sort of thing about Brezhnev without the Kremlin blowing its top."

"The Soviet Union has to learn once and for all it can't throw its weight around without paying a price," he insisted. "It would serve Brezhnev right if he got the kind of verbal abuse that would leave his ears ringing for a month."

"But I still don't know if a full-scale invasion, some artillery bombardment and air coverage by the latest jets merits the kind of relation you're talking about.

"Saying the Soviets greeted the new year by welcoming in the past or suggesting the Communists are an albatross with the Ancient Mariner around their necks is pretty heavy stuff.

"If Mr. Clark claims Brezhnev can get support in the Soviet Union only by saying, 'Elect me and I'll quit,' you know it will bring back the Cold War and escalate the international arms race."

"That's the chance we'll have to take," the hawk agreed, "but if we believe in freedom and non-intervention in another country's internal policies, we have to risk it."

"I don't know if you've thought of it," I responded, "but what if Brezhnev retaliates by repeating the Clark jokes Trudeau has been telling in the election campaign?"

"Surely the Russkies aren't that cruel," he replied.

January 23, 1980

Goodbye, goodbye to humble pie: It's a Liberal feast again

THE LIBERALS have returned to power after nearly nine months in the wilderness and, according to a party friend of mine, it wasn't a moment too soon.

"It's been hell being humble all that time," he confessed, "going around pretending we were just like everybody else, giving the impression we didn't know how to run things better than the Conservatives.

"If I showed humility once in the past nine months, I must have shown it a dozen times. Some days I thought my face would crack if I gave one more shy smile or hung my head in another display of modesty."

"I'm sure it was quite a strain for Liberals everywhere," I said. "They aren't accustomed to being out of office like the Tories or NDP."

"Exactly. When you've given orders as long as we have, it isn't easy to turn around and start taking them without any training. Being governed isn't the Liberal way of life."

"I can imagine it was pretty traumatic."

"Unless you're a Liberal, you can never understand the torment of going to a public function and watching somebody else stand up to deliver the speech, cut the ribbon or announce a new policy of some kind.

"It hurts down deep. I don't know how many times I picked up the newspaper and saw some stranger's picture on page 1 meeting a foreign dignitary or going into 24 Sussex Dr. I don't mind admitting some nights I cried myself to sleep.

"When you can't even name a friend to the Senate or an important commission, well, let me just say it's rough and an experience I'll never forget as long as I live."

"How did you handle it?"

"Like other Liberals, at first I pretended it was all a bad dream and would soon go away. But ultimately I had to face the truth and accept the fact the country was being run by non-Liberal persons, that even Bryce Mackasey didn't have a $90,000 job to his name.

"That's when we realized we might never be in a position to be arrogant again unless we pulled up our socks and did something about it?"

"Did you go humble cold-turkey?"

"Yes. We realized there could be terrible withdrawal pains and there would be time when every fiber of our being cried out for one more petulant display, one more sneer, one more curt wave of the hand to show our displeasure.

"But we also knew that would be the end of us. If we ever hoped

131

to open another stretch of highway, ride a government jet or swim in the Prime Minister's indoor pool, again we had to abstain from any sort of high-handedness."

"There must have been moments when you wondered if you could go through with your roles of good loser."

"Of course. Frankly, the darkest moment came at a Liberal meeting when someone intimated the Conservative government could go on for as long as a year, perhaps even 13 or 14 months.

"Fortunately, the budget defeat came shortly after that and we could see the light at the end of the humility tunnel. If we could live with non-power for a little while longer, our ordeal would be over."

"I don't know if it's crossed your mind," I said, "but the Liberals have been out of office 272 straight days, counting holidays. Do you think you'll remember how to be cocky?"

"That's something we'll find out after the coronation," he replied.

February 20, 1980

Chapter 9:
Resurrection

With the mess Tories left, will poor Liberals need time?

THE LIBERAL government has been in office a week and many Canadians are wondering why more hasn't been done about inflation, energy prices, natural unity and the other great problems of the day.

"You've had seven days and nothing's happened," I complained to a Liberal contact. "What's holding you back?"

"Under normal circumstances there would be full employment by now, we'd have an oil agreement with Alberta, the Quebec problem would be a worry of the past and prices would be back to 1960 levels," he replied, "but . . ."

"But what?"

"You can't believe the mess we inherited from the Conservatives. We knew things were bad in Ottawa but we didn't realize how bad until we took office.

"It's going to take longer than we thought to straighten things out. If you saw the size of the national debt the Tories left us, you wouldn't be so impatient."

"Bad, eh?"

"Even I had to rub my eyes when I saw the figures. We had all sorts of programs to get the economy moving again and we're going to be forced to put them off because of the fiscal nightmare the previous administration left us."

"They've really painted us into a corner."

"I suppose you're not the first Opposition party to feel that way when it takes over."

"Perhaps not, but I don't think anyone has ever faced the kind of economic hole the Conservatives dug for us. Frankly, our hands are going to be tied until we reduce the debt willed us by the Clark administration."

"Didn't you have an inkling of what you were in for?"

"No. We foolishly believed there would be a healthy balance in the nation's bank account and that there would be funds to implement our programs.

"However, when you're out of power, you don't really know

what is going on. Well, we've really learned our lesson. We're not going to take anything for granted in the future."

"What particularly shocked the Liberals when they took over the government?"

"I don't know where to begin. When we opened the books, we reeled from one item to the next—the growth of the bureaucracy, the cost of unemployment, the sad state of the Canadian air force, the balance of payment deficit.

"But it all gets back to the same thing—the mismanagement of the previous government. What a headache they handed us!"

"I realize I'm putting you on the spot but how long do you think it will take the Liberals to get the country's finances in order again?" I asked.

"Don't hold me to it but it could be 10 or 15 years," my Liberal contact confided. "Why, do you realize when we assumed power from the Conservatives last week, the national debt was $2,175 for every man, woman and child in the country?"

March 10, 1980

Canadians aren't quite ready to parle the Frenglish language

IF PRIME MINISTER Trudeau has his way, Ontario will become an officially bilingual province with French and English having equal status in the courts, Legislature and so on.

Some time ago I mentioned that many Ontarians have taken some French in high school but not enough to be totally fluent in the language of Voltaire and Brigitte Bardot.

The answer, I suggested, might be Frenglish, a mixture of the two.

Unfortunately, the idea didn't catch on, but yesterday I decided to give it another try, this time with a friend of mine who came back from his holidays with a beard.

"Ho, ho, ho," I began, "avez-vous une beard ou mangez-vous des Shredded Wheat?"

He replied it was a beard.

"Avez-vous perdu un bet sur les Argos? Avez-vous besoin de 99 cents pour un Bic disposable? Est-ce que vous jouez Santa Claus dans un church pageant?"

My friend denied all suggestions and said he had grown the beard at the cottage because he had always wanted one. Besides, at 43 it was one of the few ways left for him to rebel against society.

"Votre missus, aime-t-elle le fuzz sur votre chin?" I wanted to know. "Vous ressemblez à un porcupine et c'est possible que ça tickles quand vous embrassez avec passion après lights-out."

So far there were no complaints, he answered.

"Très bien. L'amour est très difficile si la femme n'est pas serieuse. Après tout, l'homme n'est pas fabriqué de stone; il a des feelings, aussi.

"Permettez-moi une autre question: Lorsque vous mangez ou buvez, est-ce que la beard interfère avec la soupe, le bifteck, la Molsons, etc.? Personne n'aime une beard qui drips."

The beard, so I was informed, occasionally trapped bits of food but that was a small price to pay for fulfilling a lifelong dream.

"Je suppose que tout le mond vous pose cette question: Lorsque vous dormez, est-ce que vous placez votre beard à l'exterieur de la Hudson Bay blanket ou est-ce que vous la tuckez underneath?"

"Underneath," was his quick response. "But I speak only for myself. I don't know what other beard growers do."

"Bon. Je suis certain, une beard est cosy dans l'hiver quand il fait si froid les brass monkeys mêmes sont nerveux. No question. Mais quand vous pouvez fry un oeuf sur le sidewalk, la beard est un drag, n'est-ce pas? Aussi, je pense que les whiskers itch comme heck tous les jours."

My friend agreed beards had a good side and a bad side but, to date, the good outweighed the bad and he was going to keep it for the time being.

"Qu'est-ce que c'est que le major problem avec votre beard? Les pigeons qui désirent faire un nest dans votre tempting under-brush? Les smart-alecks qui tirent les strands pour vérifier ils sont légitimes et not un Monsieur Freddie fake? Les jeunes filles qui

pensent que vous etes Kenny Rogers et demandent un auto-
graphe?"

"No, the biggest problem to date is trying to figure out what
you're saying," he said.

Perhaps Canada isn't ready yet for Frenglish.

September 11, 1980

How to protect the innocent

MANY CANADIANS see the current Ottawa-Alberta dis-
pute as a personal feud between Prime Minister Pierre
Trudeau and Premier Peter Lougheed. The two obviously aren't
fond of each other.

Unfortunately, they are dragging the rest of us into their
argument and, before it ends, a lot of innocent people could get
hurt.

Surely there must be a better way. I think I've got it.

Trudeau and Lougheed should meet in a winner-take-all series
of events to decide on a fair price for Canadian oil.

Both men are pretty macho; they're both proud of their physical
abilities; and Lougheed's youth advantage would be offset by
Trudeau's edge in experience and size, making for an even match
up.

But most important, the rest of us wouldn't get a bruise from
our safe place on the sidelines.

A list of possible events could include:

☐ A foot race across the swimming pool at 24 Sussex Dr.

☐ A roping competition at the Calgary Stampede, with each
competitor going against the clock to determine who takes the
least time to bring down and hogtie Stanley Knowles of the NDP.

☐ A banister-sliding event to be held at Buckingham Palace,
provided Royal consent can be obtained.

☐ A mountain-climbing test to see who can reach the peak of
Mount Lougheed in the Rockies first without supernatural assistance.

☐ A marathon disco at a smart New York city night spot where the last man standing after gruelling hours on the dance floor with a series of stunning nymphets in slit skirts will be declared the gold medallist.

☐ A passing competition in which Lougheed and Trudeau will be asked to alternately quarterback the Toronto Argos and try to complete a forward pass against the Edmonton Eskimos. First one to make a completion will win but if no one has come close after two weeks, the event will be declared a draw.

☐ A test of strength to determine who can chin himself more often on Rene Levesque.

☐ In a test of nerves, each man will be asked to stand still while Premier Bill Davis of Ontario stands at 30 paces and attempts to shoot a non-filter-tip cigarette out of their respective mouths. Marks will be taken off for flinching.

☐ A jumping event in which Trudeau and Lougheed will be asked to clear a pile of all the nasty statements they've made about each other in the past six months.

☐ A tag team wrestling match to be staged at Maple Leaf Gardens with John Crosbie acting as Trudeau's partner and Senator Keith Davey making up the other half of Lougheed's team.

The 10 events—perhaps called the decathalon of destiny—could be held over a three-month period and televised. No appeals would be permitted, of course.

And the winner, as mentioned, would have his way on Canada's energy policy.

My idea may not be perfect but it would at least get the rest of us out of the crossfire.

November 5, 1980

Poor PM! There's just no pleasing some newspapers

WITH SOME newspapers, Prime Minister Pierre Trudeau can do no right. In fact, we have two of them in Toronto—

the Globe and Mail and the Sun.

Their motto seems to be, if you can't say something bad about the PM, don't say anything.

Frankly, it must be hard keeping up a stream of criticism day after day. Being negative takes a lot out of anyone. However, I decided to put myself in their place and give it a try.

Just for fun, I put down some brief story outlines, and attempted to come up with the kinds of headlines the anti-Trudeau press would use with them.

This is the best I could do.

Story: Trudeau is walking down a street in Ottawa when he sees a small house on fire. From a second-storey window, two little children with tears streaming down their cheeks are calling for help. With no thought for his own safety, Trudeau rushes into the burning building and saves the children and their parents!

Headline: Trudeau deprives youngsters of chance to attend orphans' picnic.

Story: While attending the opening ceremonies of a sports complex in Calgary, Trudeau is invited to try out the trampoline. He does a couple of somersaults to the applause of spectators who tell reporters they are amazed at his dexterity.

Headline: Trudeau flip flop leaves westerners gasping.

Story: Trudeau dresses up in a Santa Claus outfit and makes a tour of hospitals where he hands out candy canes to all the little patients in the children's ward, taking up the better part of a day.

Headline: Dentists claim Trudeau action could cause serious health problem.

or . . .

Headline: Sweet-talking Trudeau shows old touch with suckers.

Story: One weekend, Trudeau is puttering around the basement at 24 Sussex Dr. when he spots a dust-covered lamp in a corner. He rubs it and a genie appears and offers him three wishes. Trudeau thinks about it for a minute or two and then makes his three wishes: (1) for world peace (2) for an end to starvation and suffering and (3) for a cancer cure.

Headline: Trudeau ignores west again.

Story: For the first time in her reign, Queen Elizabeth decides

139

to hold a press conference at Buckingham Palace and make known her views on the Canadian constitution patriation question. In the course of a 90-minute, questions-and-answers session, Her Majesty endorses Trudeau's policy and urges all Canadians to give him their united support.

Headline: Queen looks radiant at first-ever press conference.

And, finally:

Story: It is the year 2039. Pierre Trudeau is celebrating his 120th birthday when he hits his head on the side of the pool at 24 Sussex Dr. after executing an amazing series of difficult dives. A doctor is called but he is too late. Trudeau is deceased. His body is taken to the Rotunda in the Parliament Buildings where it lies in state.

Headline: Trudeau plot suspected—PM may be going for breath-holding record.

December 3, 1980

What gift should Peter give Pierre?

EVERYBODY has someone on his Christmas list who is very hard to buy for, but no shopper in the nation faces a bigger challenge than Alberta Premier Peter Lougheed, who hasn't a clue what to get Prime Minister Pierre Trudeau this year.

In fact, Lougheed called in his top adviser this week and laid out the dilemma. "I still haven't bought anything for Prime Minister Trudeau," he said.

"Have you any suggestions?"

"I take it you want something that reflects the way you feel about Mr. Trudeau," the aide responded.

"Exactly. When Mr. Trudeau opens my present, I don't want him to have to guess about our relationship."

"How about two tickets to the next Winnipeg Jets hockey game?"

140

"I don't think two Jets tickets says adequately what I think of the Prime Minister."

"How about season tickets for the Jets, plus a pair of seats on the 50-yard line for the opening game of the Toronto Argos' 1981 season?"

"That's getting closer, but I'd like something more, well, something that tells Mr. Trudeau how I feel about Ottawa, his federal budget and energy price offer."

"We could gift-wrap 10 shares of Massey-Ferguson stock."

"Yes, that's possible."

"How about pulling a few strings and sending him a gift certificate that can be turned in at the Stratford Festival for a seat on the board of governors?"

"Heh, heh, that isn't bad, although I'm not sure that would cause Mr. Trudeau's face to react exactly how I want on Christmas morning when he opens my present."

"A volume of the collected humor of Finance Minister Allan MacEachen in imitation leather might be in the spirit of your friendship, or else a house lot in Cayuga. Some Chrysler options are another possibility."

"Now you're talking," Mr. Lougheed encouraged, taking down the gift ideas.

"A pair of factory-second downhill skis, an all-expense holiday to Mount St. Helens for its next major eruption, a flattering character reference signed by Chairman Mao's widow, a chance to invest in Michael Cimino's Heaven's Gate . . ."

"Yes, yes."

"Skating lessons from Dan Maloney, the first home cassette version of Robert Altman's Popeye, a Nehru jacket once worn by Joe Piccininni, a year's free hair stylings from Carol Pope's own hairdresser, a croquet mallet from Conrad Black's personal set with instructions what to do with it, the battle plans drawn up by Ayatollah Khomeini for the war against Iraq, Ben Wicks' latest book—with the last chapter left in!"

Premier Lougheed gave out a hearty, "Ho, ho, ho! At last I'm getting the Christmas spirit. Frankly, I was beginning to think I'd never find something for Mr. Trudeau and would have to settle for a non-loosening necktie, but you've come up with some good suggestions.

"Now all that's left is for me to send the Prime Minister a turkey."

"You're sending Mr. Trudeau a turkey, too?"

"Of course. What's Christmas without a turkey?"

"How big a turkey would you like to give him?"

"I don't know. What would you say Marc Lalonde weights?"

December 19, 1980

Pierre must pine for his paperwork

ACCORDING to a Toronto Star report, Prime Minister Pierre Trudeau "threw up his arms in exasperation" yesterday when he learned he'd have to ski one more day at the snowbound Austrian vacation resort of Lech rather than get back as planned to the nation's business.

Of course the hearts of all Canadians, even those in Calgary, went out to the PM, trapped as he was in the Alps, totally cut off from paperwork, telephones and inviting energy debates.

Life at the top of the Alps may not be hell, but it's at least heck.

Put yourself in Mr. Trudeau's sad place.

You're planning to leave for a nifty 10-hour conference with some African head of state about heavy machinery purchases or soybean tariffs, followed by a 12-course official dinner at which goat innards are the main dish, and at the last minute you find you can't go because of yet another 18-inch fall of best powder.

Wouldn't you be crushed and throw up your arms "in exasperation"?

Sob!

There you are, dressed in sharpest blue business suit, shoes polished to mirror finish, Countess Mara necktie in place, heavy briefcase filled with important papers in one hand and vital Certs with 30-minute protection in the other.

And then it's all cancelled because of more snow!

I can see the scene.

The PM is looking out the lodge window at the snowflakes coming down as an aide rushes up to him with the tragic news: "Mr. Trudeau, you can unpack and sit in front of a roaring fire in the main chalet for another 24 hours or take another run down Devil's Elbow if you want.

"We can't get out today."

The color drains from the PM's cheeks as if some unseen hand has pulled a plug on a main artery. "Do you mean it's impossible to leave by car, train, plane, helicopter or dog team?"

"I'm afraid that's right."

"But this is the third straight day we've been trapped here. Are you suggesting I have to go another 24 hours without listening to critics of my oil policy, defending Bank of Canada skyrocketing lending rates, or talking to Finance Minister Allan MacEachen?"

"Yes."

"What about Rene Levesque, Peter Lougheed, Sterling Lyon, Brian Peckford? Can they reach me if they try?"

"Even Barbara Frum can't get you until the roads are cleared, the landing strip ploughed or the railway tracks shovelled. You might just as well go down to the dining room and have some Tyrolean stew, a glass of wine, perhaps an apple strudel, and make the best of it."

"It's inhuman. How long can a person take living in a luxury resort, sleeping under one, no more than two, down comforters, facing miles of world-class ski runs with nothing under your belt but a bowl of thick soup, a loaf of fresh baked bread, cheese, a sacher torte and perhaps a Viennese coffee? At this very moment Alberta separatists may be making devastating statements or there could be another unconfirmed rumor about Margaret's next book, and I wouldn't know about it.

"For all I know, a petition from organized labor could be waiting for me on my desk in Ottawa even as we talk. A delegation of native people could be burning me in effigy in front of the Parliament buildings and I'm missing it."

"Get hold of yourself, sir. We may be able to get you out by snowmobile but somebody's taken the spark plugs."

"Excuses, excuses. Oh well, I might as well change and get out to the tow while conditions are perfect."

On his way to his room, Mr. Trudeau opens a window and "throws up his arms in exasperation."

Nobody sees two spark plugs fly through the air and disappear into a 30-foot snowdrift.

January 7, 1981

Pierre's in for a surprise

LET ME tell you, Prime Minister Trudeau throws a very nice party. This is being written, sort of, Saturday morning, about 14 hours after the PM (do you notice how familiar I've become after just one bash?) had about 300 of us into the Chateau Laurier for a little din din in honor of West German Chancellor Helmut Schmidt. The economic summit and all that, you know.

It was all pretty grand—lobster pate, a great huge pig brought in on fire on a stretcher, fancy rice, mashed carrots, papaya with some kind of sauce, salad, kiwi fruit in custard served in a pastry shell, three kinds of wine—German white, French red, and Canadian champagne.

Of course it tasted even better because the grub was all listed on the souvenir menus in French. Don't you find that always makes it sound special?

I mean, I said "pig" two paragraphs back but on the card it was listed as "Le marcassin flambe en portefeuille de table" and the lobster pate was "Le gateau de homard du coulis de queues d'ecrevisses."

Take my word for it, even the Toronto Star cafeteria does not have items like that chalked up on the daily bulletin board. Too bad. Wienies and beans, if done up in French, would probably taste twice as good.

But back to the dinner.

As mentioned last time, I don't know how I got on the guest list but there I was at table (No. 10) with a surgeon from Brampton, an academic from the University of Manitoba and an official from the Austrian consulate in Toronto, a businessman from. . . well, there were eight of us at the table.

Of course when you go to affairs like this (now that I've been to one, I've become an expert, of course, in true journalistic fashion), you automatically assume everybody in the room is important. Why else would Pierre (yes, getting more familiar all the time) invite her, or him?

So Jackie and I gawked around trying to pick out celebs and did see the usual political faces—Jean Chretien, Allan MacEachen, Ed Broadbent, Donald Macdonald, Jeanne Sauve, Pat Gossage (who is the Prime Minister's press secretary) and so on.

In the pre-dinner cocktail party, I dare say I rubbed shoulders, etc., with some real biggies. It was very impressive thinking the person jostling my arm and spilling orange juice down my front probably was one of the 100 most important people in Regina, or has the biggest Telefunken outlet in all Calgary.

In the hope someone from Barrie was looking at me and speculating I might be somebody, I did my best not to look like a person who had driven to the Toronto airport in a '71 Canadian Tire and come in from the Ottawa airport on the bus.

But I must say Mrs. Lautens looked absolutely terrific. No wonder. Just an hour or so before we left for Ottawa Friday, we went out and shopped for the finest dress a credit card can buy. We settled on a peach number and made the plane with exactly four minutes to spare.

Unfortunately we were a little rushed at the other end, too, and Mrs. Lautens disappeared without explanation just before we went into the state dinner.

When I asked where she had been, Jackie said out in the hallway, pinning up a bit of the plunge in her new neckline with a safety pin. Well, ask a Hamilton Beach girl a straight question and you get a straight answer, unfortunately.

"When I bend over, too much of me shows," she said coolly.

"Didn't people see you adjusting your dress?" I asked in some shock. "You can't half undress in the hallway outside a state dinner without somebody noticing."

Jackie had an answer. Our son Stephen is working in Ottawa this summer and took us to the dining hall before leaving us on our own. Apparently he opened up his suitcoat so his mother could make the necessary adjustments behind his makeshift screen.

"Nobody saw," my wife guaranteed.

Already Mrs. Lautens is planning what to serve when we have good old Pete (you know, the Prime Minister) up to the house for dinner.

Well, after all, we owe him now.

I wonder if he'd like Jackie's Surprise. That's what Mrs. Lautens makes out of whatever leftovers she has in the fridge.

Of course she'd give it a French name. Surprise de Jackie.

July 20, 1981

Constitution comedy just a barrel of belly laughs

THOSE OF US who make a semi-living poking fun at the news were deeply saddened by yesterday's constitution drama from the nation's capital.

Frankly, we were hoping to knock off 600 amusing words about what was billed on the editorial pages as one of the great stories of our time, perhaps the greatest.

Having watched the live telecast from Ottawa, however, there wasn't a columnist, sketch-writer, stand-up comedian, satirist or revue artist who didn't immediately realize he or she couldn't come up with anything nearly as funny as the event itself.

Believe me, I love Wayne and Shuster, Second City, the Royal Canadian Air Farce, Don Harron—but not one of them could have written the script for yesterday's boffo performance.

It was the kind of show that makes a John Candy want to cut his wrist out of pure jealousy.

If you tuned in, you know what I mean when I say the constitution special had absolutely everything in the way of hilarity and hijinks—microphones that didn't work, jurists who mumbled, TV commentators who didn't know what was going on, keen political minds of every stripe claiming victory, law experts who looked as if they had just dropped their briefs in a public place.

And finally, a verdict from the Supreme Court that didn't decide anything.

Yes, after months of drama, discussion, the trading of opinions, etc., the country is right back where it started from. Har, har, har.

Personally, I am absolutely crushed and feel an inclination to hire a lawyer to sue somebody for taking away my living. Perhaps it should be a class action on behalf of all columnists with smiling pictures on top of their daily effort.

How can a person in my line of work put bread on the table if amateurs (who have regular professions to pay their bills) are going to horn in and make people roll on the ground, convulsed with laughter?

There probably aren't 15 people between Victoria and St. John's whose ribs aren't sore from witnessing yesterday's events.

Frankly, I was planning to write a piece today on how I got up yesterday morning and inadvertently put on my underwear inside out, a fact I didn't discover until later in the day with what I first considered rather risible results.

Do you think now I would dare try to raise a smirk with something so staid and ho-hum as inside-out underwear?

Do you think even I would have the nerve to describe how (after I discovered the error) I tried to change in a very small cubicle in the men's room, almost putting my foot in the plumbing in the process?

Not a chance.

In comparison with yesterday's laff riot, my little offering would be booed off the page.

What made yesterday's Ottawa show even funnier was the fact the lines were all delivered deadpan. It was as if we had 40 or 50 Charlie Chaplins staring into the TV cameras, not cracking a grin let alone a smile.

Why, oh, why, couldn't I have come up with that scenario first? With Walter Matthau as the lead, it would make a wonderful movie.

September 29, 1981

"Lady Jane could feel all resistance draining away"

Sex...Robert Redford...tight jeans...Brooke Shields... bosom...free offer...low-cut blouse...

None of the above is involved in today's item, but I knew if I started with "Supreme Court" or "constitution"—the real topics—you would turn away immediately to the biorythm chart to see if you were on an emotional high today.

And let me give you fair warning, I will resort to every trick in the columnist's book to keep you reading to the last sentence.

Okay, the Supreme Court ruling on the constitution won't make many people totally happy, except, of course, lawyers hired at $1,000-a-day to interpret the thing.

But the one item that especially caught my attention was the one about provincial approval.

Sophia Loren...black knickers...garter belt...giggle, giggle...

The nation's top jurists said while it wasn't legally necessary for Ottawa to have provincial backing to patriate the constitution, traditionally it was the proper thing to do.

However, the lads in the black robes backed off when it came to specifics. They didn't say how many provinces would have to say "aye" to make it all lovely and proper.

Would a simple majority do the trick, say six provinces out of 10? Would seven be better? Well, nobody knows, and the Supreme Court isn't saying. We just have to guess.

With the wind rattling the shutters of the 18th-century castle, Rupert stood in front of the crackling fire, eyes glowing with passion. He swept Lady Jane into his arms with one powerful motion and pressed his lips against hers. She could feel all resistance draining away...

But is a number count of the provinces enough?

Here is how the population of the provinces stacks up approximately: Ontario, 8.6 million; Quebec, 6.3 million; B.C. 2.7 million; Alberta, 2.2 million; Manitoba, 1 million; Saskatchewan, 978,000; Nova Scotia, 857,000; New Brunswick, 710,600;

Newfoundland, 585,800; P.E.I., 125,000.

All right, supposing for the sake of argument, Ottawa gets the support of six provinces on a big issue—P.E.I., Newfoundland, N.B., N.S., Saskatchewan and Manitoba.

And supposing four provinces oppose—Ontario, Quebec, Alberta and B.C.

From a population standpoint, that means approximately 4.3 million people would win over 19.8 million Canadians.

Please imagine a very cute pup (a cocker spaniel perhaps) being held by a winsome child of 3 or 4 in this space. The pup is licking the youngster's face.

Would the Supreme Court consider that right and proper—six provinces (with 4.3 million population) having the votes to carry the day over four provinces (with 19.8 million citizens)?

Should P.E.I. have the same clout (to be specific) as Quebec in the constitution debate? What is the Supreme Court's ruling on that?

If Quebec and Ontario got together (ha, ha,) against the other provinces, that would be a 2-8 provincial breakdown, but the pair with a total of 15 million population would constitute a popular majority. What about that?

It's too bad the Supreme Court didn't say.

Question: Is it true the birds in Hamilton (Ont.) are so dumb they go west for the winter? Answer: No. And stop telling Hamilton jokes in a cheap attempt to keep readers from straying. Pooh, pooh.

September 30, 1981

In the name of peace . . .

WITH ALL THE war talk in the newspaper this week, I've decided to do something controversial—a peace story. At the risk of offending the pro-war lobby, I've jotted down some of the nice things about peace.

Peace is quiet. Peace doesn't cause bleeding.

You don't have to wear a prickly uniform or go around saluting somebody you don't like to wage all-out peace.

Peace doesn't blow the roof off your home or make deep holes in the road.

Peace is considered a very good environment for raising children.

Peace lets you spend Saturday night at home watching the hockey game on TV, or sitting on the chesterfield in the front room kissing somebody you like.

You can wear flowers to peace.

Peace doesn't make you line up for a tin of bad meat and a hard biscuit.

The air in peace is better.

In peace you can let your hair grow, wear yellow, chew gum, forget about making the bed, slouch, quit your job, take a shower alone, hang a shirt up crooked on the hanger, stay out of tanks that shake your insides and give you a headache from the heat.

The hours in peace are shorter.

Peace doesn't make strawberry ice cream cones almost impossible to get.

Peace doesn't make you say your name backward to a lot of strangers who want you to add "Sir!" at the end of every sentence.

You don't have to crawl on your belly under barbed wire in the rain to practise for peace.

Peace doesn't hide a lovely sunset behind a big, ugly mushroom cloud.

If you lose in peace, you can read about it in the next day's newspaper.

The worst thing peace planes do is lose your luggage.

According to most medical reports, peace nerves are not a common ailment, except among Toronto Argo fans.

Peace leaves all the streetlights on so you can get around at night without bumping into buildings or falling down steps you didn't see.

In peace you can pick your friends.

An elderly politician can send a bunch of young people off to peace without their mothers and fathers crying at some train station or airport and wondering if they'll ever see their children again.

There's no embarrassing physical for peace, or age limit.

150

According to insurance company actuarial tables, people live longer waging total peace.

You can always tell what season it is in peace because peace doesn't burn the leaves off trees or cause the temperature of the neighborhood suddenly to go up 4,000 degrees.

Peace offensives don't interfere with TV reception.

Peace-ravaged countries have the highest standard of living.

If you send a young person out on peace manoeuvres about the worst injury he can pick up is a hickey on his neck.

Finally, nobody ever said peace is hell, which is worth remembering.

October 23, 1981

NOTE: No major political figure worked harder for the cause of peace than Pierre Trudeau in his last months in office. For many Canadians this was "his finest hour" and so it seemed fitting to end the collection with this column.

Epilogue

As Pierre, or Prime Minister Trudeau as I call him, leaves 24 Sussex Drive, undoubtedly the question gnawing at his vitals is this: Now that he no longer occupies the highest office in the land, will the nation's press deprive him of the advice so lavishly showered on him in the past 16 years?

If he goes on to a life in the musty halls of academe, or to some awfully important job in the international arena, will the men and women with pass BA's in sociology and Eng. Lit. who occupy our press galleries ignore him? Will they be cruelly silent when he's trying to solve some monetary crisis, or deciding whether or not it's too early to buy Michel a two-wheeler, the one with Italian gears and racing tires?

I can't speak for every member of the belles lettres gang hunched over his or her word processor but I promise I'll never desert Mr. Trudeau. I'm no fair-weather buttinski. Heck, since 1968 whenever I've needed a few bucks, all I've had to do is bat out 600 words of advice for the PM and—voilà—a nice envelope of crispies.

The Lautens maison boasts end tables, thirsty bath towels, a dishwasher with energy-saving capacity—all courtesy of Mr. Trudeau, at least indirectly. If our son Richard didn't get home early from class today, we have a refrigerator just bursting with Mr. Trudeau's groceries. And it's no coincidence the yard at our cottage at St. Sauveur des Monts in the Laurentians is affectionately called Trudeau Park by our family. We know which side our French stick has been buttered on.

So Mr. Trudeau can count on me, no matter what challenge he tackles next, no matter where he goes, no matter what high office he occupies. And I'm sure most Canadian commentators agree. We will be there, looking over his shoulder, letting him take the first guess but prepared always to volunteer the second. Whether it's a comment on what he's wearing or a few paragraphs about his latest dishy date, Mr. Trudeau won't have to ask. (He is a proud man.) The journalists of Canada will be ready.

How will our largesse be greeted? Perhaps this personal anecdote will show you, dear reader, how much the Prime Minister depends on the press and how we have been a comfort to him.

Not long ago my wife and I were invited to the world première of *Quest For Fire*, a major cinematic event (as it was billed), to be followed by a lavish reception at one of Toronto's best hotels. The Prime Minister, the invitation said, would be in attendance.

Purely by chance, as I walked into the reception following the screening, the Prime Minister spotted me and waved me over.

"How did you like the film, Gary?" he asked, standing in the midst of a small gathering of people who obviously weren't regular shoppers at Honest Ed's or even K-mart.

"Not much," I responded quickly. "I was really bored. No dialogue, just a lot of grunting. Frankly, if we hadn't been sitting in the middle of a row, we'd have got up and left."

The Prime Minister listened intently as I plowed on, showing no reaction except (so my wife claims) the slightest flickering of his eyebrows and perhaps the tiniest shaking of his head. Finally I stopped for a breath.

"By the way, Gary," he managed to edge in, "have you met Sherry Lansing, the president of the studio that made *Quest For Fire*?"

I'm sure it is a great comfort to Mr. Trudeau to know he will still be able to count on that kind of help no matter where the future takes him—or should I say, us.

June 4, 1984

154